KV-011-681

Running Your Own

MAIL ORDER
BUSINESS

Running Your Own

MAIL ORDER
BUSINESS

Malcolm Breckman

REVISED EDITION

KOGAN
PAGE

First published in 1987
Reprinted with revisions 1988, 1989
Revised edition 1992

Apart from any fair dealing for the purposes of research or private study, or
criticism or review, as permitted under the Copyright, Designs and Patents Act,
1988, this publication may only be reproduced, stored or transmitted, in any
form or by any means, with the prior permission in writing of the publishers, or
in the case of reprographic reproduction in accordance with the terms of licences
issued by the Copyright Licensing Agency. Enquiries concerning reproduction
outside those terms should be sent to the publishers at the undermentioned
address:

Kogan Page Limited
120 Pentonville Road
London N1 9JN

© Malcolm Breckman 1987, 1992

British Library Cataloguing in Publication Data

A CIP record for this book is available from the British Library.

ISBN 0-7494-0831-6

Typeset by DP Photosetting, Aylesbury, Bucks
Printed and bound in Great Britain by
Clays Ltd, St Ives plc

Contents

Foreword

by Colin Richards, Chairman (1985–89), British Direct Marketing Association

The mail order industry in the UK today is big business – and it's still growing. From art galleries to office suppliers, boat makers to garden centres, large and small companies alike are using mail order to sell their products, increase sales and acquire valuable new customers. Similarly, business people and consumers alike are waking up to the pleasures and benefits of shopping by mail.

For anyone who has ever dreamed of starting their own business, mail order represents a golden opportunity. One of retailing's major success stories, Virgin Records, was started by Richard Branson selling discount records off the back pages of *New Musical Express*! Yet for every successful mail order company, large or small, possibly another ten or twenty may have failed or gone out of business because of lack of forethought, insufficient planning or failure to understand the particular requirements of the mail order business and the market they were operating in.

In *Running Your Own Mail Order Business*, Malcolm Breckman has produced an invaluable and immensely practical guide which will be essential reading for anyone thinking about setting up their own mail order business. Packed full of useful advice and tips, the book guides the reader through the ins and outs of the mail order market in an entertaining and down-to-earth way.

Introduction

This is a book for beginners, certainly for those new to mail order, probably for those also new to business. It's for people who, looking for a business opportunity, have suddenly thought in the *eureka!* manner – 'Hey! What about mail order?'

Mail order looks fascinatingly simple to outsiders, like a money-making machine. You can scarcely pick up a national paper or periodical that doesn't include mail order ads somewhere in its pages. No one spends advertising money without hoping for a profit, so presumably profits are being made. And presumably also if *you* ran ads like those, you'd also make a profit. If only you could find someone to tell you which buttons to push, and show you where the money comes out.

Perhaps the first hint you get that mail order is less straightforward than it looks is when you talk to the experts. 'Mail order?' they tend to say, looking slightly pained. 'Mail order? What exactly do you *mean* by mail order?' It comes as a bit of a surprise to discover that everyone knows what mail order is except those in the business.

This book aims to explain what mail order consists of, to show the complexity behind the simplicity, to give an insight into the business, to suggest how it might be approached on a limited budget, to survey the whole range of matters that anyone seriously contemplating the business needs to know of and understand, to help you decide if it's a business for you, and to point you in the right direction if you think that it is. But forget about money-making machines. They don't exist.

Chapter 1

Mail Order for Beginners: Doddle or Disaster?

Mail order looks easy. You put an ad in the paper or some letters in the post, orders drop through your door, you pack a few parcels, mail them off to your customers, call in at the bank to pay in the takings, then back home to the telly and the champagne.

No prizes for guessing that that's an over-simplification. And yet mail order does seem to offer beginners a number of genuine advantages compared with other forms of trading. Your mail order business may not, at first, need special business premises: you can operate from home. You don't need to work special hours: the postman drops the orders through your door whether you're in or not. You may be able to start off in mail order without having to give up the security of your regular job on someone else's payroll: it makes no difference whether you work on your own business at 10 in the morning or 10 at night. You may be able to get started with a relatively modest amount of capital: you can take your first tentative steps into the business with a small stock of a single low-cost product.

Mail order also looks attractive as a way of developing or improving an existing business. If you're a shopkeeper, for example, regularly rushed off your feet at certain times, while at others you've almost nothing to do, then you may have wondered whether mail order might not be the answer to your problems. Overheads mount up as relentlessly when you're idle as when you're busy: rent, rates, insurance, heating, lighting, and so on, remain at their same high level whether you happen at the time to have a dozen customers in the shop or none at all. Mail order work slotted into the slack times might enable you to increase your turnover while holding your overheads steady.

So both for the beginner and for the person already in business, mail order looks an attractive proposition, apparently offering a low-commitment way of getting into business or developing an existing one. How does the reality square with the appearance?

Mail order looks easy but isn't

While all the favourable points mentioned above are indeed true, they're not the whole truth. Mail order looks easy only because the publicly visible part of the operation seems so simple: put an ad in the paper and you're in business. But press advertisements are by no means easy to create, can sometimes be difficult to get accepted for publication, are certainly not cheap, necessitate a prior investment in stock which in turn may give rise to the need for borrowing, warehousing and insurance, and at the end of the day, they may fail to cover their costs by a very wide margin. And most of the same is true even if you bypass the press and send your advertising in the post. So certainly not a doddle.

On the other hand, mail order business, large and small, plainly exist, continue in existence from year to year, and may therefore be supposed to be trading profitably. All of them were newcomers once – so success can't be impossible to achieve. Mail order may not be a doddle, but it needn't be a disaster either.

From time to time, you hear mail order hyped up as a fantastic opportunity for business beginners. It isn't. Repeat. It isn't. Mail order is a business activity like other business activities. It has some advantages that other forms of trading lack, but equally it has disadvantages that they're not burdened with. A postal strike, for example, which may be no more than a major nuisance for most businesses can mean extinction for the small mail order business. On balance, there's nothing special about mail order as a business opportunity. Don't go into it in the belief that profits can be made easily, quickly or in vast quantities. They can't.

In mail order, as in all businesses, the small beginner is invariably at a disadvantage because of his lack of experience, understanding and – probably – money. Time brings experience; the present book offers at least the beginnings of understanding; it's money, of course, that's likely to be the major handicap. If you've got enough of it, you can hire all the experienced and knowledgeable people you need to get your business soaring into fully fledged existence. But if money is tight, you will have to proceed slowly and cautiously, learning as you go by trial and error.

The sensible approach

In mail order you can begin in a very small way. It's quite possible for someone working single-handed, or perhaps with just one or two others, to start and run a small mail order business. It can be done with little capital and without previous experience. That is not to say that it is easy to launch a successful business in these circumstances, but it is possible. Regard any small, low-capital venture into mail order as in the nature of an experiment, a toe in the water, a means of researching possibilities with a view to exploiting them on a larger scale if the experimental results are promising.

The possibility of entering the business cautiously and with minimal risk is one of the attractions of mail order compared with other forms of trading. You couldn't, for example, open a bookshop with only one title in stock, or a hotel with only one bedroom. But there is no problem in beginning in mail order with a single product, only adding others on the basis of experience in the market-place.

Indeed, this tentative, experimental approach to mail order is the only sensible one for the beginner to adopt. And not only the beginner. An important characteristic of mail order is that it lends itself to experimentation; it is almost always possible to try things on a small scale before taking risks on a large one. The established traders do it all the time; and so should you.

Keeping your options open

In its experimental stages, mail order is flexible in a way that other business ventures are not. If you try selling computer software, for example, and the results are poor, you can switch to selling digital watches or religious books or ladies' underwear or whatever. You can even try more than one line of goods at the same time. Flexibility of this sort is not to be enjoyed in most other forms of trading. No shopkeeper, for example, can stock out his shop with computer software, see how it goes for a couple of months, and if things aren't looking too hopeful, clear everything out and try his luck with religious books on one side of the shop and ladies' underwear on the other.

Note, though, that the advantage of flexibility in mail order is lost if you make too large a stock investment in untried products. It will be no use discovering with your first few advertisements that there isn't, after all, a demand for table-top concrete mixers if you have a warehouse crammed full of the wretched things. Mail order gives you the chance to experiment on a small scale: don't throw that chance away.

Maximise non-business income

If it's possible to do so, continue in full-time employment while experimenting with your mail order ideas. Or get a job – any job – that will give you enough to live on and so delay the time when your new business will have to support you.

Enterprise Allowance schemes

Various schemes sponsored by government, national or local, offer help to people intending to set up in business on their own for the first time. The help generally takes the form of business counselling, advice and training, and a regular allowance paid for a limited period. The exact terms of the schemes vary from time to time and place to place. They are usually targeted at people who are between the ages of 18 and 65, who have been unemployed for several weeks, and who have a sound business plan and an amount of capital to invest in it. For details of available schemes, contact your local Jobcentre.

Minimise business expenditure

The main way of doing this is to work from home (unless, of course, you can use business premises you're already paying for in another business activity). There is little point in incurring the expense of long-term business premises until you are confident that you have a long-term business to accommodate.

It is also prudent, as already said, to keep stock levels as low as possible. Don't make a large investment in stock merely to obtain trade terms or a large discount. In the early stages of your venture, it is far more important to identify profitable forms of trading than it is actually to make a profit. It could even make sense for you – for the purpose of testing the market – to buy your initial stock at retail prices. Of course, you are bound to lose money this way, but once the test results are in, you can work out what your profits would have been if you had purchased at trade prices, and so decide if it's worth buying wholesale in order to continue the operation on a larger, and this time profitable, scale.

Stock levels: a warning
You might think that the sensible thing to do would be to buy no stock at all until you have actually received orders from customers, and then to go to your local supplier and buy the precise quantity you need to fulfil those orders. You couldn't get a lower stock risk than that.

But that system is emphatically *not* to be recommended. Reputable papers will only accept mail order advertising from traders who hold adequate stock to meet a reasonable response from readers. Without experience to guide you, it is impossible to say what 'adequate stock' amounts to, and the experience needed is not experience of mail order in general, but experience of the particular advertisement selling the particular product at the particular price. Without such experience, all is guesswork. But for want of something better, here is a very rough rule of thumb: if you're asking customers to send paid orders in direct response to press advertising, your total volume of sales from any one publication of the advertisement is unlikely to exceed six times its cost. So, for example, if you advertisement costs £50, your total volume of sales in unlikely to exceed £300; and if your product sells for £10, your 'adequate stock level' would be 30 items (ie 30 × £10 = £300).

Do be clear that this six-times-ad-cost formula is a very rough formula indeed and is only to be used in the absence of relevant experience. It is in no sense a prediction of the typical volume of sales you can expect, nor will it necessarily satisfy the particular paper in which you wish to advertise. But as a raw beginner, you may well feel that any point of reference, however uncertain, is better than no point of reference at all.

Even if you advertise only by post and so avoid the need to persuade the papers of your business bona fides, you should still aim to hold adequate stock before making any offer to the public. The danger otherwise is that when you get orders you can't fulfil from stock, and so have to go for fresh supplies to your local dealer, you might discover that the product has drastically increased in price or, even worse, is no longer available at all. Your customers will not see your blushes as you return their money, nor will the papers or the Post Office hear you gnashing your teeth as you reflect on how much you have spent to promote a product you belatedly discover you are unable to supply; but this is no way to run a business – not even a small, experimental one.

So keep your capital investment low by keeping your stock level low, but not so low that you risk being unable to meet a reasonable response to your advertising.

Draw up a budget

Even small, experimental ventures need adequate funding, and *low capital* is not the same as *no capital*. So how much will you need to get started?

Literally to get started, you need no more than the price of your advertisement and a stock of goods. Fifteen pounds will buy you a small classified ad in a paper like *Exchange & Mart*; so, applying the six-times-ad-cost formula, you also need £90-worth of stock at retail prices. But if that's all you can venture, you will need to be very successful very quickly if you are not to find yourself broke and out of business within a fortnight. You may achieve success with your very first advertisement, but the odds are much against it. You will have to be pretty lucky for your first attempt to cover its cost, let alone make a profit. You are likely to place many unsuccessful ads before you hit upon one that produces promising results, and it may be some time before you have accumulated sufficient evidence even to recognise that the results *are* promising.

If you're to make a serious attempt at setting up a profitable mail order business, you should give yourself six months at least to try out your ideas and to feel your way carefully from the almost inevitable short-term difficulties towards a longer-term success.

There are two quite separate components to your start-up capital requirements: (a) business money for advertising, stock, processing orders, general overheads etc, and (b) money for your personal survival. In the small, experimental stages of the business, it is the latter cost which is likely to be the more burdensome.

Business money
For an experimental six-month trial, running the business from home or from other premises you are already paying for, you will need to budget for at least the following: (a) advertising, (b) stock, (c) stationery, postage and packing, (d) incidentals. The exact amount of business money you need will depend, of course, upon the scale of the operation and the nature and value of the goods you are dealing in. But let us suppose that the product you sell costs you about £3, and that you intend to experiment on the smallest possible scale that might fairly test whether your business ideas contain a germ of success. The single component of a mail order operation which determines the scale of the whole venture is the amount of advertising, and you will probably want to allow yourself an advertising budget averaging £60 a week at the very minimum if you are to give your ideas a fair run.

In that case, your six-month business money budget might look like this:

		£
(a)	Advertising (26 weeks × £60)	1,560.00
(b)	Stock	500.00
(c)	Stationery, postage, packing	270.00
(d)	Incidentals	170.00
	SIX-MONTH BUSINESS MONEY BUDGET	£2,500.00

So on that showing, the amount of business money you need, and must be prepared to risk losing, is £2500 in the very smallest of serious mail order experimental ventures. Of course, you expect *some* money to come in from customers even if the experiment is not an instant success, but don't rely on having customer money to recycle; you'll feel much more relaxed if the whole £2500 is available in the bank to start with.

Not that there's anything magical about this figure of £2500. It is given here only as an example of the possible minimum you will need to try out your plans. To get a better idea of how much will be needed for your own particular venture, estimate your advertising and other costs for yourself, and draw up a simple budget on the lines of the one above. Err on the side of caution, and allow yourself enough capital for a six-month run of failure. The money won't do you any harm if the profits start coming in after only two months, but the knowledge that you have reasonable capital will give you the confidence to help you meet and overcome any early reverses. In this, as in all businesses, the more money you have, the longer you can stay in business, and the longer you can stay in business, the greater your chance of success.

Remember also that we are here talking of the business money you need to *experiment*, to give yourself a fighting chance of discovering a profitable mail order formula which will allow you to operate your business successfully. Once you have such a formula, further capital will be needed to scale up the size of the operation – the amount depending entirely upon your business ambitions at that point. You will by then, however, have hard evidence on which to base your calculations, and if that evidence genuinely points towards a profitable future, you should have a strong case to present to your bank manager if you need additional funds to get the business on to a sound footing.

Money for personal survival
Ideally, you will have an independent income. But if you haven't, then you'll have to live off your savings. Work out how much you'll need over the next six months. The surest way to calculate that is to see how much you spent in the last six months.

Get out your bank statements, building society pass books etc and work out: (a) how much money you had six months ago, and add to that (b) the total amount of money – after deductions – that you have earned, won or been given in the last six months. This gives you (c) the total amount of cash you had available over the period. Compare that total with (d) the total amount of money you have today. This will show you (e) how much you have spent over the past six months. And you are likely to need at least the same amount for the next six months if you are to continue in your present life-style.

Here is an example of what such a calculation might look like:

		£	£
(a)	TOTAL WEALTH SIX MONTHS AGO		
	Barclays Bank (current account)	274.00	
	Barclays Bank (deposit account)	26.00	
	Abbey National	10,460.00	
	Post Office savings	740.00	11,500.00
(b)	INCOME DURING PAST SIX MONTHS		
	Wages from the XYZ Co	6,912.00	
	Win on the pools	260.00	
	Inheritance from Uncle Jim	2,000.00	9,172.00
(c)	TOTAL AVAILABLE CASH OVER LAST SIX MONTHS		20,672.00
(d)	TOTAL WEALTH NOW		
	Barclays Bank (current account)	263.00	
	Barclays Bank (deposit account)	14.00	
	Abbey National	11,878.00	
	Post Office savings	120.00	12,275.00
(e)	TOTAL EXPENDITURE OVER LAST SIX MONTHS		£8,397.00

So how much to get started?

If the figures in the example budgets applied to you, the minimum total amount of capital you would need for a full-time six-month venture into mail order would be:

	£
Business money	2,500.00
Survival money	8,397.00
	£10,897.00

Near enough £11,000. Can you afford it? Look back at (d): £12,275 is your total wealth now. So you *can* afford it – but don't ignore the fact that if you try and fail, most of your savings will have been wiped out.

Again, it must be stressed that the important figures are the actual ones that apply to you for your own particular circumstances, business plans, and life-style. Only you can work them out, on the pattern of the examples above. As soon as a mail order plan starts to crystallise in your mind, calculate the figures to see what your capital requirements would be and whether you could meet them.

Are you the right sort of person for the business?

Even if you have the money, the product and the ideas, mail order may still not be for you if it doesn't suit your personality and disposition. Mail order can be a lonely activity, particularly in a small business. You never meet your customers face-to-face, are never able to indulge in friendly conversation while making a sale; perhaps, if you run your business entirely alone, you may spend the whole day without talking to a soul. Even in a larger business, with partners or staff to talk to, you are still fundamentally isolated from the customers in the market-place; you communicate with them as if you were in quarantine, only by the printed or written word or occasionally by telephone.

Whether this is an advantage or disadvantage depends upon your own character and disposition, but it is something you must seriously take into account before committing yourself to the business. If yours is an outgoing, sociable personality, if you enjoy meeting people, exchanging pleasantries, discussing, explaining, negotiating, persuading face-to-face, then there are other forms of trading that you should consider as possibly more suited to you than mail order. A shop of your own? Market trading? Party plan selling? All of these take you out into the world to meet and deal with your customers face-to-face. You must decide for yourself which sort of business activity best matches your skills and personality.

Qualities needed

The qualities needed in a mail trader on a day-to-day basis tend to be 'backroom' ones: attention to detail, methodical working, a head for figures, and the ability to deal carefully and without error with repetitive clerical and packaging tasks. If this makes it seem rather boring – well, it can be. But mail order also needs the flair of the person who can recognise a winning product and dream up the advertising and marketing approach that will get it profitably sold. Commercial success, if achieved, is a powerful antidote to boredom.

Perhaps the major quality needed is the ability to sell. Whatever the mechanics of the operation, *selling* is what mail order is all about. That's a simple but vital truth that must be faced. You can sell things in a shop, from a stall in the market-place, by hawking them from door to door, and in a variety of other ways as well. One of those is mail order. If you're not interesting in selling, then mail order is not for you.

Make no mistake about it, the essence of mail order is not packing parcels or taking money out of envelopes or designing clever advertisements that impress your friends: the essence of mail order is *selling*. And though some people at some times will be so anxious to buy what you have to sell that you need do little more than announce *I can supply XYZ*, most of your prospective customers will have to be persuaded by you to make a purchase. You won't have to persuade them face-to-face like the door-to-door double-glazing salesman but the underlying psychology of your methods will not be all that different from his.

If you're disposed to throw up your hands in distaste and say, 'I couldn't possibly *sell* anything to anyone', then forget about mail order. Although mail order is conducted, as it were, by remote control, it remains selling, and the successful mail order business is always built upon successful selling and salesmanship. Other things are needed besides, of course, but the most attractive products, the best value for money, the lowest prices, the finest after-sales service – none of these things are of any use at all unless you can *sell* in the first place.

Is it worth going on to Chapter 2?

The thing to be clear about is this: while it is relatively easy to start in mail order, it is no easier than any other business to succeed in. At bottom, mail order demands exactly the same things as any other business: money, imagination, intelligence, energy, patience, perseverance, self-reliance, the will to succeed – and luck. There is no set of rules that you can blindly follow, confident that riches will come pouring in. There are no trade secrets that ensure success, no mail order products bound to make you a millionaire, no guaranteed methods that will turn you into a prosperous entrepreneur by this time next month.

If you can accept that, read on.

Chapter 2

The Mail Order Industry

Mail order is big business. It accounts for about 6 per cent of all non-food consumer spending – something like £4620 million a year. An estimated 25 million people make mail order purchases each year, spending about £185 each. Confusingly, though, mail order is also small business. The major catalogue houses have about six million part-time agents on their books – and that makes it look as if a quarter of the working population has an entrepreneurial finger in the mail order pie.

The above figures, by the way, are based upon and have been calculated from figures published by the Mail Order Traders' Association, of which more later.

So what exactly is mail order? Big business or cottage industry? How does it work? How is it organised? Where does the serious new entrant to the business fit into the total picture?

Terminology

First, let's try to sort out some of the terms. Note particularly the meanings of the following:

Direct mail is a form of advertising. It consists of letters and/or literature sent through the post to specified individuals.

Mail order is a form of distribution. Despite the implications of the term, transactions are not necessarily conducted by post. What characterises the method is that goods or services are promoted, ordered and delivered without buyer and seller ever meeting face-to-face.

Direct marketing is another name for mail order, and is the term preferred by most people in the industry, possibly because it lacks the restrictive connotation of *mail order* noted above. Orders, after all, may well be solicited in the press, received by phone, and delivered by private carrier, *mail* having nothing to do with it at all. But while the practitioners tend to talk of *direct marketing*, the public still feels more comfortable with the term *mail order*, and that's the preferred term also in this book.

Direct response is used to describe aspects of the mail order operation, eg *direct response advertising* or *direct response selling* or even *direct response*

marketing (the latter therefore coming to the same th
marketing).

The commonest error is to speak of direct mail as if it we
as mail order or direct marketing. Make sure that you car
isn't. Direct mail is advertising. It may be used as part of a
operation, but it may equally be used for other purposes – to urge people
to vote for a particular political candidate, for example, or to invite them
to visit a newly opened local restaurant.

And yet . . .

If you pick up another book on mail order, you could well find the above
terms defined slightly – or even very – differently. This is part of the
problem, and not, by the way, a problem unique to mail order.

The difficulty arises when an existing term is felt to be not quite fit for
the current practice. A new term is invented, but no one is quite sure of
its precise scope. Some people use it one way, some another. Theological
squabbles develop as one guru says the term means X, a second says it
means Y, and a third unhelpfully proposes the use of another term
altogether. Meanwhile, down at ground level, the laity are still using the
old term and having no problem with it at all.

Perhaps there's an element of deliberate obfuscation in all of this. In
his very readable book *Commonsense Direct Marketing*, Drayton Bird,
having first said that mail order and direct marketing are *not* the same
thing though the latter encompasses the former, then goes on to say that

> . . . where once one muttered at a smart party, 'Er, mail order', when asked
> what one did for a living, one can now say loudly: 'Direct Marketing'. And
> people will say: 'How interesting. What exactly is that?'

Note also that the section on mail order in *The British Code of Advertising
Practice* (see page 78) though headed 'Mail order and direct response
advertising', talks exclusively in the text of *mail order* and never again uses
the term *direct response* at all.

If none of this has clarified your thinking, at least you can feel
comforted that the confusion lies in the general practice and not in your
understanding of it.

The nature of the business

As pointed out in the last chapter, mail order, in essence, is just a way of
selling things. It is not a business in the sense that estate agency is a
business, or watch repairing or bookselling or car dealing, each of which
specialises in a certain type of product or service. Mail order is simply a

21

ay of selling. There are no special mail order products; mail order is a method not a product.

So what can be sold by mail?
Almost anything. If you doubt that, just peruse the pages of mail order ads in a paper like the weekly *Exchange & Mart*, where you'll find everything on offer from bumble bees to balaclavas.

Nor is mail order restricted to the selling of goods only. Many services use this method of selling. Much insurance, for example, is sold this way – motor insurance, hospital and sickness insurance, insurance-linked unit trusts, and so on. There are some building societies which operate almost exclusively by mail, and an increasing number of other financial services are marketed this way. All sorts of prize competitions are conducted by mail – football pools and product promotions, for example – as are correspondence courses in a wide variety of subjects.

None of this is to deny that some things are particularly suitable for mail order selling just as others are particularly unsuitable. But what matters is not the inherent nature of the products or services themselves but the cost of the mail order operation – advertising, postage, packing etc – relative to the cost of the thing being sold. For example, a can of beans selling for about 30p in a high street shop might cost you more than a pound in post and packing if you wanted to send it through the mail. The disproportion of product cost to mailing cost rules out single cans of beans as mail order possibilities. No one will pay £1.30 by mail for a product he can get without difficulty for a fraction of the price in a local shop.

Mail order, then, cannot compete on equal terms with other forms of selling. For something to have a chance of selling successfully by mail, it must usually have a favourable difference from anything obtainable in the local high street. The difference may be a lower price, or something unique about the article itself, or it may be something special about the terms of the offer – a free gift, perhaps, or favourable credit terms, or a chance to buy further goods at a privileged price – but without such a difference, you are likely to fail, however good the product or the advertising.

The structure of the industry

The UK mail order industry is composed of giants, tiddlers and everything in between. It is useful to have a picture of the industry as a whole to get an idea of where your own proposed activities might fit in.

Catalogue houses

The majors

The major catalogue houses publish large, attractive catalogues of as wide a range of goods as you will find in a city department store. The catalogues are supplied free to agents, usually housewives recruited through advertising in popular journals, who promote the goods to friends and neighbours, send off the orders, and collect and forward payments due. An important feature of this kind of mail order is the availability, with minimum fuss or formality, of simple credit terms from the catalogue houses. The agent needs no business capital to get into this sort of mail order, but she is unlikely ever to make more than a little pocket money for her efforts: typically she gets a commission of between 10 and 15 per cent of the sales she makes. For most women the main attractions of an agency are personal: it adds an interest to life, gives the agent a chance to meet more people more often, and effectively enables her to buy goods for herself at a discount.

Indeed, in recognition of this last point, the companies are increasingly dispensing with the agency concept and are providing their catalogues and marketing their goods direct to the individual purchasers.

The major catalogue houses, though trading under a variety of names, are in fact no more than a handful of holding companies. Yet they account for about 80 per cent of UK mail order business, and their turnover is reckoned in thousands of millions of pounds. When you hear people talk about the boom in mail order, this is where it's happening.

The minors

These are catalogue houses which have never sold on the agency principle. Their catalogues attractively present a range of goods, tending towards the gadgets and gimmicks end of the market (see below). Whereas the catalogues of the major mail order houses are often hefty tomes running to a thousand pages or more, those of the minor catalogue houses generally slip easily into a C5 envelope, and are normally direct mailed to prospective customers or even given as handouts in shops connected with the mail order companies.

For beginners?

No. Being an agent for one of the major houses might give you an interesting hobby but it won't put you seriously in business. And an attempt to enter the minor catalogue house market would require a very substantial capital commitment and a highly professional marketing organisation to have the remotest chance of success. This is not the place for the beginner to try his luck.

Mail order departments

These are often run by shops and stores which are not primarily in the mail order business at all. They produce catalogues for mailing to their regular customers, and much of their postal business is from past personal customers who for reasons of time or distance are no longer able to shop in person.

For beginners?

If you already have a shop, particularly if it is one that attracts a large number of customers making one-off purchases – perhaps because it is in a tourist area with a seasonal trade – you may be well placed to develop a mail order offshoot. You could give your personal shoppers catalogues of your products to take away with them, complete with information on how to buy from you by post. You could also contrive to get the names and addresses of personal shoppers – perhaps by offering to send them, say, a free Christmas catalogue – and in this way build up a mailing list. It's likely to be a long, slow business, but if your products are suitable (see the next chapter) this sort of mail order requires relatively little capital investment, and may in time grow into something of value.

The mail order department operation has three crucial advantages over the pure catalogue operation.

First, your *prospects* – that's the shorthand jargon for your prospective mail order customers – have already done business with you, and therefore, we hope, they know that they like your products and they have confidence in you as a trader.

Second, your promotional costs are limited to catalogue production and mailings to a few well qualified prospects. You don't have to buy in lists or undertake expensive press advertising.

Third, no substantial stock investment is required as the things you offer in your mail order catalogue are already in your stockroom for sale to personal shoppers. If the mail order side of the business thrives, well and good: total turnover increases, stock orders can become larger, unit costs therefore probably fall, and ultimate profits rise. If the mail order side fails, no great harm will have been done: you always have the option of selling off in your shop – at knock-down prices if need be – any surplus stock you laid in for mail orders which never came. A mail order venture of this kind almost has an insurance policy built into it, provided you're patient enough to let the business develop from within rather than try to force the pace by undertaking mail order advertising to non-customers.

Mail order discount firms

These are often run in association with cash-and-carry warehouses or shops very barely fitted out and offering minimal service. Low prices and cut prices are their main selling features, and their advertising frequently stresses the savings possible in a mail order purchase compared with one made in the high street. A lot of their business is in branded goods, which allow the easiest price comparisons, and audio, video and electrical goods feature particularly prominently in their sales. The success of such firms depends upon large stock purchases, quick turnover and low overheads.

For beginners?
If you're already running this sort of warehouse business profitably, then it could be worth adding a mail order component. Otherwise not.

Specialist mail order firms

These cater for particular interests: stamp collecting, archery, aids for the disabled, model car components etc. Mail order is particularly suitable for such firms because there are few areas of the UK where the local level of interest and demand can support a specialist shop of any size. A mail order firm, however, can trawl for business across the whole of the country.

Specialist mail order firms usually advertise in the appropriate specialist papers, though their long-term commercial strength lies in their mailing list of customers, slowly built up over the years.

For beginners
If you are knowledgeable and expert in the speciality, this is an area of the mail order market which you might seriously consider. Of course, you will first want to check out the size of the market, the availability of suitable advertising media to reach it, and the nature of the present competition. It is, however, a definite possibility.

Manufacturers selling direct to the public

It is popularly believed that by cutting out the retailer, and – where he exists – by cutting out the wholesaler too, the manufacturer can market his goods both more cheaply to the public and at a greater profit to himself. It must be borne in mind, however, that if he bypasses the middlemen, he has to provide within his own organisation the services they normally provide. And that costs money too.

For beginners?
Manufacturing is a very different activity from retailing. If your

expertise lies in the former, you will normally find it best to concentrate your efforts there, leaving it to those skilled in retail distribution to shift your product on to the general public.

If you've tried marketing your product to wholesalers and retailers but they've shown no interest in taking it, ask yourself honestly whether the product is genuinely saleable in its present form, at its present price, at the present time, to the present public. Middlemen don't normally decline the chance of making money, and if they won't handle your product, there's probably something wrong with it. Think very carefully before launching yourself into an area of business, as a raw beginner, in an attempt to retrieve a failure in a line of business where you are genuinely expert. Mail order can't sell the unsaleable.

There are two circumstances when, as a manufacturer, you might consider mail order. First, if the product is of a specialist nature, with too few retailers of sufficient size and skill able to handle it effectively. Second, if your research has revealed a gap in the mail order market – an area of demand currently unfulfilled – which you believe your manufacturing skills could supply. There's a world of difference between manufacturing a product to fit a gap you have confidently identified in the market, and desperately scrabbling to find a market for a product you're already stuck with.

The gadgets, gimmicks and novelties mail order firm

This is what the general public tends to think of – incorrectly, as we have seen – as the typical mail order business. Firms like this rely almost exclusively on continuous press advertising, usually using *bargain square* advertisements – one column wide and an approximately equal heights – each devoted to a particular product. The total number of products they deal in may run into hundreds or it may be only one.

For beginners?

This is one of the more visible areas of the market and the one to which many beginners naturally gravitate. Indeed, it does provide one of the quickest and cheapest ways for the newcomer to 'have a go': quickest, that is, if you can get the press to accept your advertising (see Chapter 5), and cheapest, which is not the same as cheap, at, for example, a VAT-inclusive £235 in the *Sunday Telegraph* (1992 rates).

With one product and one ad, you can put a toe in the water. But what then? The message coming back from the toe will almost certainly be that it's decidedly chilly out there. Regrettably, any dreams you might have had of being overwhelmed by orders from your single advertisement are unlikely to be fulfilled. See Dave Pattern's comment below on typical response rates.

The difficulty for such businesses is how to develop any real business momentum, ie to build up a body of regular customers and so escape the stranglehold of expensive press advertising. The people fascinated by your folding walking-stick may not by turned on by your pocket solar-powered radio or your plastic Christmas tree. Follow-up sales (see page 51), the jam on the mail order bread, are not easy to achieve.

Making money in mail order

Although overheads like rent and rates tend to be low compared with other retail businesses, other costs – advertising and postage, for example – tend to be high. Just as the shopkeeper needs to maximise his sales per square metre of floor space, so the mail order dealer has to maximise his sales per pound of advertising money. How does he do it?

Press advertising

Press advertising, even in a specialist paper, is like trying to hit an invisible target by spraying shot in all directions. You know the customers are out there somewhere, and you hope that the law of averages will take some of your shot to its target. But it's a very inefficient and expensive procedure: masses of shot and a tiny number of hits.

In his book *Successful Marketing for the Small Business* – very well worth reading, even though mail order is not central to its theme – this is what Dave Patten has to say on the subject of response to press advertising:

> I recently carried out my own research on the pulling power of the Sunday 'Postal Bargains'. A dozen advertisers were canvassed. I picked out what looked like newish small firms, asking for the response to their ads. The replies seemed to average around 30 per insertion. The moral is clear: don't be deceived by massive circulations.
>
> From a readership of perhaps 3 million with a circulation of 1 million perhaps 100,000 actually saw the ad. Of those, perhaps to 90,000, it was of no interest. The remainder either had one already, thought it too dear or didn't like the colour, were saving up for Christmas and would get round to it 'one day'. Maybe 500 decided they would like one but forgot to look out some writing paper or the husband lit the fire with that issue. Thirty wrote for the brochure and 10 actually bought one. And there are bound to be one or two who returned the product.

Just reach for your calculator and work out what that means. If the advertising space cost, say £235, and eight sales were achieved, then each sale cost the advertiser getting on for £30 for the newspaper space alone. Depressing, isn't it? The figures are not *always* as bad as this, and there are indeed companies that consistently make profits from press advertising, but it isn't easy and no one has yet devised a formula that guarantees success.

Direct mail

Though most mail traders have to use press advertising some of the time
– and new traders particularly may need to – for many, the preferred
form of promotion is direct mail, in which advertising is posted to
individuals on a mailing list. Lists may be composed of one's own past
customers or enquirers, or be compiled by research, or be rented from list
owners who have themselves built them up in one or other of these ways.
The random spray of shot is now replaced by the sniper's bullet.
Provided the lists have been intelligently compiled and maintained, this
is a much more efficient procedure. Even so, response percentages very
rarely get into double figures: a 2 per cent rate is fairly typical if you're
using a good rented list. Get out your calculator again. With second-class
postage at 18p and enclosures costing, say, 10p, and another £70 to rent
the list, then 1000 items cost £350; a 2 per cent response, therefore, means
that you make 20 sales, for each of which you have spent £17.50 in
advertising. Not cheap, but better than £30.

A strategy for mail order

For most businesses, the mailing list that produces the best results is their
own list of past customers. And this fact lies behind the most widely
pursued strategy in mail order: to build up a list of customers. Because
this is where the most profitable business promises to be, it is not unusual
for firms to accept a short-term loss on their press advertising, which they
regard less as a way of selling goods than of 'buying' customers from
whom future profits will be made.

Aha!
This is often the explanation of something that baffles and dejects many
mail order beginners. You place an ad which seems to you very similar
in its appeal to one that another mail order company has been running
for months on end – and yet your ad fails and loses money. How, you ask
yourself in some bewilderment, do *they* make their advertising pay?

There are a number of possible positive answers. A mail order
campaign is made up of many parts, of which the press advertisement is
only one. Two seemingly similar ads may thus form part of two very
different selling operations, and this makes it impossible to explain the
success or failure of a particular ad by reference only to the ad itself.
Account must be taken also of all the concealed costs which only the
advertiser himself knows about: general overheads, purchasing costs,
staff salaries, and so on.

If you are trying to copy the supposed success of another advertiser,
you will need to duplicate *every* aspect of his mail order operation,
including those which, short of espionage, you simply can't know about.

You may both be selling a well-known brand of Thingummies at exactly the same price from virtually the same advertising in the same paper; but if he is purchasing his thingummies direct from the manufacturer at £2 each while you are getting yours from a local wholesaler at £3 each, he may be making a small steady profit while you are making a small steady loss.

But the likeliest explanation of the other advertiser's continued presence in the advertising columns is that though his ad doesn't pay in the short term, it does pay in the long term. Perhaps he encloses a catalogue with all orders despatched, his profits coming from the sales that the catalogue produces. Perhaps he direct mails his customers every six months, his profits coming from that operation.

This is the point: the iceberg tip of mail order advertising that you are familiar with as a member of the public is just the visible fraction of a complex selling operation, the ultimate profits of which may arise only indirectly and after the passage of time.

Support services for the mail order industry

A variety of agencies provide services to the mail order industry. Again, the terminology can be confusing. They are variously referred to as *advertising agencies, mailing houses, fulfilment houses, direct mail producers, producer houses, lettershops, direct marketing agencies* and other things besides. Once again, the scope of any of these terms is by no means clear, and anyway, one service tends to shade imperceptibly into another. Not all agencies provide all services; those that do are generally spoken of as *full service agencies*.

The range of services available

It is probably helpful to consider the nature of the mail services provided rather than the labels attached to those who provide them. When you come to need any of these services yourself, approach an appropriate association from among those listed later in this chapter and seek their help in finding a suitable agency.

Creativity and design
The creation of all forms of advertising and advertising literature, and the preparation of artwork for printing or publication.

Fulfilment
The warehousing and despatch of goods on behalf of the mail order advertiser.

29

Letter printing

The production of personalised letters by *matching in*, ie putting an individual's name and address in the usual position in an otherwise pre-printed letter. Some agencies can also produce letters that look individually typed throughout.

Mailing

Folding, collating, inserting, sealing, address labelling, pre-sorting (see page 153) and finally posting direct mail items – in short, the physical side of the mailing operation.

Mailing list services

Computerising. While all the agencies offering mailing list services use computers, there are some *computer bureaux* for whom the provision of computer services is a central rather than an incidental function.

List building. Compiling a new list to the client's specification.

List broking. Bringing together the owners and users of particular mailing lists – which are normally the customer or enquirer lists of particular mail order businesses or the membership lists of particular organisations – so as to provide a rental income for owners and fresh markets for users. And also, of course, a commission for the broker. Brokers can normally provide fairly standard lists off the shelf, eg lists of accountants, doctors, lawyers etc, and they will actively seek out and negotiate the rental of any specific lists the client requires.

List management. Putting the client's list on computer, checking for and removing duplicate entries, checking that addresses are correct, adding postcodes where missing, adding or removing names on client's instruction and from Post Office returns (ie undeliverable items because the customer has moved or died or the address is wrong), coding the entries for selective mailings etc.

Print buying

While some agencies have their own in-house printing facilities for advertising and promotional literature, the expertise of others lies in knowing who can do the best and most cost-effective work for any particular printing job. Using the middleman skills of the print buyer can often get you better quality at a lower price.

Space buying

Space here means advertising space in the press. Agencies normally receive a commission from the media for advertisements they place on behalf of clients, so they can make available to clients their knowledge of the media and their skill in negotiating good positions without making a specific charge for the service. The client pays the same for the advertising space whether he books it direct or through a recognised agency. Of course, other services provided by the agency are charged for in the ordinary way.

Trade associations and other influential bodies

There are a number of organisations which influence, monitor and to some extent regulate the mail order trade in the UK. Some are concerned exclusively with the mail order trade or aspects of it, while others have a wider remit which takes in mail order as one responsibility among many. Most of the trade associations have codes of conduct which members are required to abidy by. These codes have normally been prepared in consultation with the Office of Fair Trading, and are frequently closely modelled on the two codes which are published by the Advertising Standards Authority.

Indeed there is a good deal of cooperation between most of the organisations listed below. They tend to regard each other as colleagues rather than competitors. Some are members of each other's organisations; and even when the relationship is not as close as this, the officers of different bodies frequently work together on committees dealing with matters of common interest.

You should have at least a nodding acquaintance with the role of each of these bodies. Some, whether you like it or not, may concern themselves with your affairs from time to time. Others may be able to help you with advice or information, but the initiative and approach will have to come from you. Others again are worth knowing about for the completeness of the picture, even though you may never have anything to do with them at all.

The organisations are listed below alphabetically. You will find addresses and telephone numbers in Appendix 2. Please note that the comments that follow are not intended to be comprehensive statements of the organisations' aims and functions, but only of those aims and functions that are relevant to the independent mail order trader.

Advertising Association(AA)

The AA is a federated body representing advertisers, agencies and the media, as well as numerous marketing and research associations, advertising services and consultancies – a membership of some 2000 in all. Many of the organisations listed below are members of the AA, which is not itself an appropriate association for individual traders. The

AA's Information Centre, however, deals with enquiries from non-members.

Advertising Standards Authority(ASA)

The ASA is the advertising industry's own policeman. The standards it expects advertisers to observe are set out in *The British Code of Advertising Practice (BCAP)*, Section C.V1 of which directly concerns the mail order trade. It also publishes *The British Code of Sales Promotion Practice (BCSPP)*, which may concern some mail order dealers. (See page 78 for more details of the Codes.) Though it has no legal powers of enforcement, the ASA is so widely supported by the major practitioners in the field that any trader whose advertising incurs its displeasure may have little choice but to change his ways or shut up shop.

The Code of Advertising Practice Committee (CAP)

Though produced under the general supervision of the ASA, both *BCAP* and *BCSPP* are in fact the work of CAP, which is also responsible for monitoring UK advertising and promotions and for adjudicating between disputing advertisers.

CAP's day-to-day work is looked after by the CAP Secretariat, which is always on hand to advise intending advertisers and others whether the content of an advertisement or sales promotion is likely to offend the Codes. Advice is both free and confidential. A phone call may be enough to deal with relatively simple problems; more complex ones are better submitted in writing. Either way, CAP's advice, though valuable, should not be regarded as conclusive; someone may still find something to complain about. Seeking advice from CAP, however, will help you avoid many of the pitfalls and alert you to problem areas you may not have thought of.

Direct Mail Information Service (DMIS)

The DMIS is the largest independent source of data and market intelligence within the UK direct mail industry. Extract reports on specific issues are published on a regular basis and are distributed to agencies, advertisers and suppliers. The DMIS was formerly operated by the now defunct Direct Mail Sales Bureau. It is currently operated on behalf of the Royal Mail by the HBH Partnership, a direct marketing consultancy.

Direct Mail Services Standards Board (DMSSB)

Though sponsored by the Royal Mail and the ASA, the DMSSB is an independent body dedicated to the upholding of high standards by those providing direct mail services. It is not a trade association and does not, strictly speaking, have members, but only recognised houses entitled to use its logo. In order to be 'recognised', a service company must satisfy the DMSSB that it is financially sound, has had a minimum – normally – of two years' trading experience, that it is committed to maintaining the highest standards in direct mail advertising, and that it upholds accepted codes of practice and works only for clients who do likewise.

Its freely available *Handbook of Recognised Agencies* gives the following information for each firm: name, address, telephone number and fax number; when founded; number of employees; contacts; parent company if any. Each entry is coded to show which of the following services are provided: design/creative, list owner, list building, list broking, list management, database management, computer bureau, printing, laser printing, enclosing/despatch, fulfilment/response handling – and for each of these, whether the service is for consumer or business-to-business activity.

Direct Marketing Association (DMA)

This is the main trade association for firms engaged in mail order, both the traders and those offering services to the traders. The Direct Marketing Association (UK) Ltd, to give it its full name, came into being in April 1992 following the amalgamation of four previously independent associations.

The names of the former associations give some idea of the scope of the new one: Association of Mail Order Publishers, British Direct Marketing Association, British List Brokers Association, and Direct Mail Producers Association. Indeed, membership of the DMA is through membership of one of its four so-called constituencies: advertisers; agencies; list brokers and database houses; mailing houses, printers and materials suppliers.

Annual membership fees (1992) range from £30,000 for the largest corporate members to £350 for sole traders with no employees except secretarial support. Between the extremes, the fee is based either upon a company's annual direct marketing advertising spend or its gross income from the supply of direct marketing services and/or consumables.

Incorporated Society of British Advertisers (ISBA)

The ISBA represents advertisers in general: its involvement in mail order is very limited. It publishes a number of booklets on advertising, has a regular neweletter, and runs workshops, seminars and conferences on advertising. It has an advisory service which member companies can use as a consultancy on advertising and communications problems.

Institute of Practitioners in Advertising (IPA)

The IPA serves and represents the major part of the UK advertising agency business, with its member agencies handling over 80 per cent of all advertising placed by UK agencies.

Mail Order Protection Schemes (MOPS) Publishers

MOPS are designed to protect the interest of readers who respond to mail order press advertisements inviting them to send money in advance for advertised products. There are five separate MOPS, each run by a different publishers' association:

- Newspaper Publishers Association
- Newspaper Society
- Periodical Publishers Association
- Scottish Daily Newspaper Society
- Scottish Newspaper Publishers Association

MOPS are of crucial importance to mail order advertisers in the press, and their scope and application is discussed in detail on pages 79–87.

Mail Order Traders' Associations (MOTA)

Although, from its name, you might suppose that MOTA is *the* trade association for mail order dealers, in fact it isn't. It is exclusively the association of the major catalogue houses – a total membership of seven.

Mail Users' Association (MUA)

MUA is an independent association of, in the main, large business users of the postal services. It aims to monitor, review, analyse and publicise Post Office policy and practice, with a view to bringing about improvements in services.

Mailing Preference Service (MPS)

MPS, sponsored by the DMA, MOTA, MUA and the Royal Mail, enables members of the public to have their names suppressed or added to mailing lists. MPS is funded by the Mailing Standards Levy collected by the Royal Mail via Mailsort contract invoices (see page 153). At quarterly intervals MPS circulates the latest list of requested deletions or additions, both of which are valuable to the direct mailer. The former produces a valuable saving on production and despatch costs of mailshots otherwise destined for the waste-paper basket, and the latter increases the size of the selected market. MPS was launched in 1983 and at the end of 1991 had a total of 280,000 names on its suppression file (surnames at address) and 12,000 individuals' names on its additions file.

The British Code of Advertising Practice requires that mailers suppress names advised for deletion on their non-customer lists.

Suppression does not apply to your own customer lists unless the customer makes a direct request to you to stop mailing him.

People who wish to have their names added to mailing lists are asked by MPS to specify their areas of interest from the following: home, leisure, clothing, financial, sport, travel, children, community services.

Members of the public who ask MPS to suppress their names from mailing lists can expect a reduction of up to 90 per cent in the mailings they receive from companies of which they are not customers.

Any company using direct mail should ensure that they use MPS-cleaned lists. If any company wishes to receive the suppression file, it can become a licensed user at a fee of £100 (1992 rates). The service is free to members of the public.

Office of Fair Trading (OFT)

The OFT is a government department headed by the Director General of Fair Trading. Its aim is to protect the consumer by encouraging competition among businesses and making sure that the consumer is not the victim of unfair practices. Its Consumer Affairs Division has three main areas of responsibility: *consumer policy* – proposing and promoting changes in law or practices where the consumer's interest is being harmed; *regulatory* – administering the Consumer Credit Act and having a role under the Misleading Advertisements regulations, among others; and *information* – providing consumers with information they require. Many of the mail order self-regulatory schemes were devised by trade associations in consultation with the OFT, under its consumer policy role, and have been endorsed by the Office.

The Post Office

The Post Office Corporation is made up of three separate businesses: Royal Mail, Parcelforce and Post Office Counters Ltd. Royal Mail is the letters business of the Post Office, Parcelforce is of course the parcels business and Post Office Counters acts as agent, through its network of some 20,000 post offices across the country, for many of the services offered by the other two Post Office businesses. Details of the various facilities offered to the mail trade by the three Post Office businesses are mentioned as appropriate throughout the book, and particularly on pages 152–153.

Post Office Users' National Council (POUNC)

POUNC is an independent body, funded by the Department of Trade and Industry, which represents customer interests in the monopoly services of the Post Office. It deals with complaints and representations from the public and businesses where customers are not satisfied with the response from the Post Office.

POUNC also has a statutory right to be consulted about proposed tariff changes and major changes to Post Office services, although the Post Office is under no obligation to amend or withdraw their proposals following representations from POUNC.

The Council maintains a watch on Post Office performance and undertakes independent research into customer requirements. It also makes proposals both to the Post Office and the government in the interests of its customers.

Chapter 3

Assessing a Product's Suitability for Mail Order

One of your first and most critical tasks as a mail trader is to decide on your product. It may be that you already know what you would like to sell, perhaps because you manufacture it yourself or are already trading it in a non-mail order market. Or it may be that you are simply attracted to mail order as a form of trading, and have as yet no product at all in mind. Either way, you need to know how to assess a product's suitability for mail order before making a final commitment.

We have already seen that it is not just the product's inherent nature that matters; remember the can of beans example (page 22). A product sold successfully by mail by a trader who runs his business from the back bedroom at home may lead to speedy commercial collapse if the business is transferred to rented warehouse premises. A good product for *you* to sell by mail may be a bad one for the mail trader next door. You must make *your* choice for *your* business. While some of the considerations that make a product suitable for mail order have a general validity, others relate to you personally and the way you run your business.

What sells?

There is nothing that sells by mail that does not also sell in the street market, the village shop, the high street chain store or in some other non-mail order way. What you're looking for is not something labelled 'mail order product' on a wholesaler's pricelist, but a product which you judge to have the characteristics that make it suitable for you to sell by mail. Partly it's a matter of the physical attributes of the product, partly it's a matter of your own circumstances, skills and knowledge in relation to the product and its marketing, and partly it's a matter of estimating whether the sums will come out right at the end of the day.

The thing can be stated in the opposite way too. Just as anything that sells by mail can also be sold in other ways, so anything that *fails* to sell in other ways is very likely to fail also to sell by mail. Mail order is *not* a device for unloading stuff that you can't otherwise get rid of. An unsaleable product doesn't transform into a saleable one just by being put into a different shop window. Remember that it's the same public out there whether they buy in person or by mail.

So what *does* make a product suitable for mail order selling?

Checklist

You should be able to give favourable answers to the following questions:

- How well do you understand the product?
- Does the product have mail order appeal?
- Can you make a unique offer?
- Is there a market for the product, and are you sure that it is large enough and that you know how to reach it?
- Can you price the product competitively?
- Is the quality right?
- Is the product's price/weight ratio satisfactory?
- Is there a satisfactory gross profit margin?
- Is there a satisfactory gross profit/advertisement cost relationship?
- How easily can the product be despatched?
- How easily can you handle the product, both singly and in quantity?
- How easily can the product be advertised?
- How difficult are after-sales problems likely to be?
- Are there attractive follow-up possibilities?

These questions are considered below, and once you have familiarised yourself with the thinking behind them, you should work through the checklist to assess *your* prospective product. In the real world, of course, perfection is rarely to be found and you may have to settle for a product which offers a preponderance of favourable characteristics even though it has negative ones also. The important thing is to get a clear idea of the product's advantages and disadvantages for mail order selling by you in your business, so that you can make an informed and intelligent decision.

How well do you understand the product?
Resist the temptation to trade in a product, however suitable it may be in other respects, if it is one that you don't fully understand. Mail order may seem on the face of it to require no more knowledge than of the way to pack and despatch whatever the customer has ordered; and it is doubtless possible, with a bit of luck, to sell things you know nothing about, provided the customers are so anxious to buy that you have only to name the product to be overwhelmed by orders for it – the mail trader's dream. In practice, however, customers rarely demand to be sold to: they have to be persuaded to buy.

Without an understanding of the product, you cannot have an understanding of the market, and without that, you are unlikely to make reasonable guesses as to what the market will buy. Once you have chosen your product, you need to know which features to highlight in your advertising and sales literature, and you need to be able to assess what your competitors – and not just mail order competitors – are selling, so as to determine how best to promote your own product. Advertising will have to be prepared, enquiries answered, after-sales problems dealt with – all requiring a genuine knowledge of the product.

Indeed, long before you come to deal with your customers, you will have to deal with your suppliers, and will need to know how to purchase wisely, and how to judge the merits of different though similar products.

A reasonable starting point in your search for a product to sell by mail is to identify an area of interest in which you have special knowledge and understanding, and then to look within that area for a product which meets the other criteria discussed below.

Does the product have mail order appeal?

Every retailer has to find convincing answers to two questions:

1. Why should the customer buy this product?
2. Why should he buy it from me?

The mail trader must additionally find an answer to a third question: Why should the customer buy the product by mail order?

Mail order is rarely a first choice

If all else were equal, most people would feel happier passing their money across a counter and being handed the chosen product in return. That way they can see what they're buying and can get their hands on it the moment they part with their money. They have no fears that the order might go astray and their money be lost, or that the goods might fail to arrive for weeks on end or be unsatisfactory when they do arrive, or, worst of all, that the offer might turn out to be fraudulent, the supposed mail order dealer vanishing with the loot without supplying anything to anyone. Despite the MOPS (see page 79), many people continue to be uneasy about shopping by mail, particularly when dealing with a new firm.

So why do people buy by mail at all? Leaving aside the few who live so remote from shops that they have no choice but to use mail order, most people only buy by mail if the particular offer made is not readily obtainable in the shops. This is the *mail order appeal*, which may be something special about the product itself or in the way you offer it for sale.

What makes mail order appealing?

There are some ways of making mail order purchases attractive that can apply to any product: a refund guarantee for unwanted goods returned within 10 days, a chance to examine the product at leisure at home, delivery of goods right to the customer's front door, and so on. Such things should always be stressed in your advertising.

Other features may relate to the particular product. If it is of your own manufacture, for example, it may be unobtainable elsewhere. Or your prices may be lower than shop prices. Or the product may be one that can be effectively tested only in the particular circumstances of home: hi-fi equipment, furnishings that must be seen in place, products that need to be used to be judged. Or the product may require regular servicing, which you guarantee to carry out, as needed, by return of post. Or it may be something that the purchaser feels embarrassed to buy in person. Again, whatever the mail order appeal, draw attention to it in your advertising. Hammer it home if appropriate, for example:

> Try our latest stretch covers on your own favourite armchairs. See how good they look! And remember, we'll send you your money back by return if you don't agree they're fantastic value.

Or, more tactfully, if *that* is appropriate, as, for example:

> For just £5 (refundable with your first order) we'll send you under plain cover our latest sensational catalogue of sexy underwear.

No mail order appeal: no sale

When deciding what to sell, consider the product's mail order appeal, and if it doesn't seem to have very much, and you can't think of how to give it more by the terms of your offer, then avoid it. Unless the customers can see clearly why they should buy the product, why they should buy it from you, and why they should buy it by mail, then they won't buy it at all.

Can you make a unique offer?

If you have a genuinely unique product that the customers want, so much the better. But truly unique products are difficult to come by, and those that achieve any measure of popularity are unlikely to remain unique for long, as the competition will produce similar products even if they can't copy yours exactly.

It is, however, less important to have a unique product than to make a unique offer – a lower price than anyone else, a chance for customers to buy further goods on privileged terms, a free gift, a free maintenance contract, and so on. You don't need earth-shattering new products or inventions to succeed in mail order; properly marketed, the old ones will do very nicely. What you *do* need is to offer your product in a way that gives it a competitive edge. A product not widely available in the shops, or one that *is* widely available but only a higher price – characteristics like these can form the basis of an offer that is unique enough for your purpose.

Beware of business beginners' kits
There is no reason to avoid selling goods similar to those of other dealers. Indeed, the existence of other dealers – if they are long established – is evidence of the existence of a market. But avoid any product specifically promoted to business beginners as being suitable for mail order selling; with such a product, bought in response to such a promotion, you would merely become one of possibly scores of new traders trying to sell the same thing in the same way to the same people. That is quite decidedly *not* unique enough for your purpose.

Is there a market for the product?
It is unwise to choose a product for which you cannot see an active, existing mail order market in the same or related items. This is the other side of the uniqueness coin. A product without competitors may also be without customers. If you have a unique product that would interest stamp collectors, for example, then – on this score at any rate – you have no problem because you will easily find a number of magazines that carry mail order advertising for stamp collectors. But where would you advertise a product for illiterate left-handed grandmothers, however useful if might be?

Need and demand
Do not confuse *need* with *demand*. It is not enough to have a product which can do many seemingly vital things if nobody actually wants to buy it. There may be a need for everyone to make regular six-monthly visits to the dentist, but there's little demand for it. Conversely, there's no need for people to eat sweets, chocolates, cakes and biscuits, since we can all survive very well without them, yet the demand for these products continues at a high level. As a trader rather than a teacher, reformer or missionary, you are concerned with demand not need, and you must choose the products you deal in accordingly.

Let other dealers make the running
In mail order, you will have enough problems to cope with without also being a pioneer – that's why you need a flourishing existing market. If you use the press, you need to be on the same page as the other traders because this is where the customers habitually browse; if you use direct

mail, you need a well maintained list of existing purchasers of products like yours. Those are the market-places – do you know where to find them?

Look in the national press, the popular journals, the hobby and special interest press, the trade and professional press, and find out where the markets are for particular types of products; consult a list broker to see if suitable lists exist. If you can't see a flourishing existing market for your proposed product, then avoid the product and look for another.

You've found a market – but is it big enough?
Once you have identified suitable markets, there still remains the question of whether they are large enough to support a business based upon the product you have in mind. Unless you are intending to mount one-off campaigns (not a good idea, see page 52) – making a big splash with a particular product for a week or two and then dropping it and switching to something different for the next fortnight and something different again for the fortnight later – the markets must be of a sufficient size to support your regular promotion of the same or related lines.

Can you price the product competitively?
There is no fixed relationship between profit and price. Consider two examples:

You buy Product A for £6 and sell it for £9. Profit: £3.
You buy Product B for £2 and sell it for £7. Profit: £5.

That elementary arithmetic is easily overlooked. Of course, you will want to think of your possible selling price as you consider different products, but you must also keep in mind the profit margin that the product offers. The selling price matters to your customers; the profit margin matters to you.

Price is a major factor in any selling operation. The lower the price, the more sales you can expect to make, though whether the increased sales lead to increased profits depends upon the make-up of the selling price. For example, if by keener purchasing you reduce your cost from £3 to £2 an item, you can reduce your selling price from, say, £9 to £8, and still make the same number of pounds profit per item sold, with the chance of increasing your number of sales. By contrast, lowering your price from £9 to £8, while still purchasing for £3, *must* reduce your profit per item, and only testing the market will show whether your lower price leads to a sufficiently increased number of sales to compensate for the reduced profit margin.

The narrow competition

As far as product choice is concerned, you must be able to price competitively, both in competition with other mail order dealers and with the shop trade. Few people will order by post if they can pick up a similar product at a similar price on a local shopping expedition.

The broad competition

Bear in mind also that you're just one of many people trying to get the public to part with its money. You're therefore in competition with *all* other traders, not just those dealing in similar products to your own. People only have a limited amount of disposable cash. Anything spent on booking a holiday in Spain is not available for buying a new wheelbarrow; anything spent on a new wheelbarrow is not available for a new pair of shoes; anything spent on shoes is not available for a crate of beer – and so on. When customers buy *your* product, they are at the same time denying themselves very different but doubtless equally appealing products from someone else. The less painful you can make this denial, the more disposed people will be to buy from you.

Easing the pain of purchase

Assure the customer that he is not making an irrevocable commitment to your product: if he finds he doesn't like it, he can return it for full refund. The money-back guarantee helps the customer to feel that he is not really making a final choice: if he is disappointed with the binoculars he buys from you, he can always get his money back and buy a digital watch from someone else.

Another way of easing the pain of purchase is by price. If the price of your product is low enough, the customer may feel it to be only an incidental expenditure that barely influences his other possible purchases at all. But how low is low? The person earning £50,000 a year will not have the same view of what constitutes incidental expenditure as a schoolgirl doing a Saturday job in the local bread shop. But most prospective mail order customers would probably consider anything under £5 as a minor outlay, and anything up to £10 as not terribly significant. That defines the price range in which it is easiest to sell.

Is the quality right?

The only aspects of quality that may be accurately conveyed in advertising are those that can be precisely measured or defined. A photocopier that produces 20 copies a minute is clearly in a different class from one that produces only two copies a minute. But that says nothing about the standard of reproduction or of the reliability of the machine. A record player with treble and bass controls plainly offers the listener more influence over the final sound than one without such controls, but it by no means follows that the machine with the controls produces the superior sound. A true assessment of quality must always be based upon personal examination. Hence the mail order problem when goods are bought unseen.

Excellence or adequacy?
Because advertising is very well suited to listing the factual specifications of a product but poorly suited to conveying an accurate idea of its quality, you should prefer a product with an impressive number of listable features rather than one which you personally judge to have a high but unspecifiable quality.

Your customers will buy on price, because that is measurable in advance; quality becomes a significant factor only after purchase – that is, in determining whether the sold goods stay sold, and whether customers are satisfied enough to make further purchases from you in the future. Just by reading the ads anyone can see that a £5 product is cheaper than a £7 product. What no one can tell from the ads is whether the dearer product is better designed, better crafted or made from more reliable materials.

What you're looking for, then, is a product which has the highest quality consistent with the lowest price. Quality and cheapness are characteristics pulling in opposite directions, and inevitably you must compromise. If very high quality means very high price, customers may never buy the product in the first place. If very low price means very low quality, you may well make a large number of sales, followed, unfortunately, by a large number of returns for refund. Somewhere between the two extremes is the target to aim for: a price that is low enough and a quality that is high enough. In other words, quality must be *adequate*. You will find that a well made item retailing at £5 is easier to sell than an excellently made one retailing at £7.

Is the product's price/weight ratio satisfactory?
The more your product weighs, the higher your delivery cost; the larger it is, the more packaging it will need. Both weight and size put up your price without putting up your profit.

Most carriers charge more for their services than the Post Office; and the Post Office has a rate scale that increases with weight, and a maximum weight for parcels of 30kg. For higher weights than this you are obliged to use non-Post Office carriers. One way or another, the heavier your product, the more it will cost to despatch.

Whether you separately identify delivery cost in your advertising or embody it in a so-called delivery-free product price, it forms an important element in the mail order calculation, and it must be considered at a very early stage in your product search.

Ideally, delivery cost should be only a small addition to the product price – preferably not more than about 15 per cent – if it is not to put customers off. The higher the price of the product, the less you need to worry about weight; the lower the price, the more important it is.

Note that it is *price*/weight ratio that matters, not *cost*/weight ratio. It can well happen, especially if you are the manufacturer, that the cost to you of the product is lower than the cost of shipping it. That doesn't matter. The figures that have to be weighed against each other are the price the customer pays for the product itself compared with the amount he has to pay to get the product delivered.

Is there a satisfactory gross profit margin?

Most people new to retailing experience a mild shock when they first learn the prices at which goods change hands within the trade compared to the prices at which they are sold to the public. It seems that traders must be making fortunes. Typically, for example, a book selling in the shops for £9 may be available within the trade for £6, or a TV set selling for £250 may have a trade price of no more than £180. With such profit margins, the beginner is tempted to believe he could make his first million in a year at most. It isn't so, of course. The profit margins illustrated above, though fairly typical, are only *gross* profit margins. The trader's real profit – his *net profit* – is not the simple difference between his selling price and his buying price, but between his selling price on the one hand and his buying price, advertising costs, rent, rates, wages bill, stationery, postage, insurance, heating, lighting, telephone, accountancy, bank charges, interest charges, equipment purchase and maintenance and other overhead costs on the other.

The 3:1 ratio

The new mail trader operating in a small way, and possibly running his business from home, may be spared some of these costs, but advertising and shipping costs alone can be heavy, and the gross profit margin must be large enough to cover these costs and still leave a net profit. The conventional wisdom is that about a third of the mail order selling price is needed to meet the cost of advertising the product. This means that just to break even on your advertising, you probably need a 50 per cent mark-up – that is, a selling price half as much again as your buying price. For example, buying for £6 and selling for £9 will at best allow you to cover your advertising costs but nothing more. Buy for £6 and sell for £8, and you can confidently expect to lose money.

This is, of course, a crude generalisation, and any actual set of results may contradict it. But in the absence of specific evidence with a particular product, earmark a third of your selling price to pay for your advertising.

What sort of gross profit margin, then, are you looking for? Again, the generalisation is crude, but something like a two-thirds gross profit margin is desirable if you are to have a realistic chance of making a net profit. One-third of the selling price, as already suggested, will hopefully cover your advertising cost, and another third will cover everything else and give you a chance of being left with a profit.

For example, if you're buying for £6, you must consider selling for not less than £18. That may look like an enormous profit, but it isn't. Most of the 'profit' will go in paying for the promotion, processing the enquiries, and fulfilling the orders.

It comes to this: your selling price will probably need to be not less than three times your buying price if you are aiming to make an immediate net profit from your advertising. This is the 3:1 ratio to keep in mind as you assess likely products. If you're thinking of dealing in Whatsits, and they are typically being retailed at £12, you can see at once that you can't afford to pay more than £4 yourself. And again: if you manufacture something yourself for £10, you will probably need to sell it for £30 or more to have a chance of making a profit, and if £30 looks ridiculously high as a retail price – well, back to the drawing board.

Is there a satisfactory gross profit/advertisement cost relationship?

The cost of a given advertising space in the press or of a given number of direct mail shots does not vary at all with the profit margin of the product you are selling. A bargain square in your favourite daily paper, for example, costs exactly the same whether your gross profit is £5 per item sold or £30 per item sold.

Your customers, of course, neither know nor care about your profit margins, but if you aim at a two-thirds margin as discussed above, it follows that a higher priced product yields a greater absolute profit than a lower priced one. For example, two-thirds of an item selling at £9 yields £6 whereas two-thirds of an item selling at £6 yields only £4. With advertising costs fixed, you have to sell a larger number of low-priced items than of high-priced ones to cover your costs.

Prices down = sales up: prices up = sales down

The countervailing consideration is that – once more as a generalisation – the number of sales you can reasonably expect decreases as your selling price rises. Assuming people are interested in your product in the first place, you will get more buyers if you sell at 50p a time than if you sell at £5 a time.

But this inverse relationship of price to sales is not mathematically precise or predictable. Even if you offer your product absolutely free, you will still only get a finite number of takers: after all, there are only a certain number of people who read the paper or receive your mailshot, and only a percentage of those will be interested in your offer. So no matter how low your selling price, you will never push your number of sales beyond a certain threshold. And from that it follows that too low a gross profit, even if it *is* two-thirds of selling price, must lead to failure.

For example, suppose your advertising costs you £100, while the unit cost of your product is 10p and your unit selling price 30p plus postage. With a gross profit margin of 20p per item, you will need to sell 500 items to cover the cost of advertising alone, and perhaps a further 500 to cover overheads and to show a net profit. Such a number of sales for a £100 advertisement is highly improbable.

How many sales can you expect?
It is easy to see what is required, much less easy to achieve it. You need to pitch your selling price at a level which not only produces an adequate gross profit relative to your buying cost but is also one which is adequate relative to your advertising cost. In the absence of experience, you cannot know how many sales a given advertisement can produce at a given price, but until you have that experience, assume that your number of sales is *unlikely to exceed* the number of pounds you spend on your advertisement, and this irrespective of your selling price per item.

This is yet another crude rule of thumb, offered for your use only until you have actual experience and actual results to guide you. So, for example, assume that a £100 advertisement will produce *at most* 100 sales, and possibly, or even probably, far fewer, depending upon the appeal of your offer and the selling price. If your gross margin of two-thirds would not adequately cover your advertising cost, overheads and desired net profit on a sale of 100 items, then pitch your price at a different level or look for a different product.

How easily can the product be despatched?
Packing your product to withstand the rigours of transmission through the postal system or other carriage service is an important element in your mail order operation. Poor packing may lead to an unacceptably high level of transit damage which in turn will lead to complaints, returned goods and the erosion of your profits. Packing which is so secure and perfect that no damage ever occurs may be very costly in terms of packing materials, time taken to pack, and increased shipping charges

because of added weight or size, again leading to the erosion of your profits. Some products come individually packed by their manufacturers in outer cases suitable for shipment with little or no extra packaging needed. Carefully consider whether your chosen product will present problems in this area.

Letter post v *parcel post*
Products light enough to be packed for mailing in the second class letter post – ie not weighing more than 750g – are usually the easiest to despatch: just drop them in your nearest letter-box any time of the day or night. Even this simple operation, however, can have snags if you fail to make some elementary checks in advance; letter-box mouths vary greatly in size and some will not accept anything much larger than a 230mm × 160mm package without folding. Don't assume that just because your product packs to a letter-box weight that it will necessarily be postable in all letter-boxes. You may have to travel some distance to find a box that will accept your product; alternatively, you will have to hand it over a post office counter. Either way, your product may cause you more inconvenience than you had at first imagined.

Items for the parcel post must normally be handed over the post office counter, though Parcelforce collects parcels from the premises of customers who have entered into a Parcelforce Standard Contract. Royal Mail offers a free collection service for letter post items when a thousand or more letters are posted at the same time.

For items you don't send by post, you will have to use one of the many other carriers. Look for possible carriers in Yellow Pages and check their rates and terms before committing yourself to a particular product.

How easily can you handle the product, both singly and in quantity?

The items that make up the stock will either have to be collected by you from the supplier or delivered by him to you; if you are a manufacturer the same will apply to the raw materials you use. To make collections or take deliveries, you will have to arrange to be available at particular times or you will have to entrust someone else with the task. Different products present different problems. A stock of cheap jewellery items, for example, may be dropped through your door in a small postal packet, while a stock of typewriters may come in a large delivery van whose arrival date and time cannot be predicted. Warehousing, similarly, may be no more than a drawer in the sideboard or may need a substantial floor area with fixed shelving and racking.

Some items are light and easy to handle; others are heavy and cumbersome. The minimum amount of handling any product can have is first when it comes into stock and second when it is despatched to the customer. In practice, however, you can expect to handle stock more than this. Items may need to be rearranged for convenience and efficiency as stock levels run down. Preparation for despatch may need additional packaging, perhaps also requiring the combining of the contents of separate cartons or the splitting up of a single carton. Have you the physique, the stamina, the time, the equipment and the working space to handle your chosen product?

How easily can the product be advertised?

The nature of some products may be clearly indicated simply by naming them, eg wellington boots, wine bottles, handbags, loft ladders, watering cans, and so on. Other less common products may need lengthy descriptions. If you have invented a device, impregnated with an anti-flea chemical, which is fixed by screws to a wall, and which is so shaped and has such a pleasing smell that cats love rubbing themselves against it to have a really enjoyable semi-automatic de-flea-ing scratch, how would you describe that in one or two words?

If, for example, you were selling handbags, you could run a classified advertisement reading something like *LATEST HANDBAG CATALOGUE free from Hannah's Handbags etc.* But how would you advertise the cat-scratch device? *LATEST CAT SCRATCHER: free details from. . .?* Even in the columns of a cat lovers' magazine, that would be unlikely to excite much interest. To bring out the real nature of the product would require many more words and probably illustrations too. Whether it is a matter of added words or added pictures, the result is the same – added cost.

Since advertising is likely to be the small mail trader's largest single expense, it is sensible to try to have a product that can be advertised simply. This means not only that you should have a clear idea of where the product may be effectively advertised, as searching for suitable places by a random process of trial and error can be a very costly business, but also that you should have a good idea of how the product may be advertised in the minimum space, with the smallest number of words, and the simpliest kind of illustrations – if any.

Favourable characteristics

The simplest thing to advertise is a well-known branded product at a bargain price. If Moggs Model K Personal Stereo is selling at £50-£60 in every hi-fi shop in the country, mail order advertising in the classified columns of the hi-fi press need to be no lengthier or more complicated than *MOGGS MODEL K PERSONAL STEREO by return of post. Only £39, post free.*

Most products, however, will require more verbal description and sometimes visual illustration as well. The more unusual your product, the more difficult it will be to describe it briefly or illustrate it cheaply. If you are committed to mail order selling, keep in mind from the start the special problems of where and how to advertise, and don't take on board a product that is likely to need full-page colour supplement advertising if your funds only run to more modest promotions in the hobby press.

Most of all, look for a product with a prime selling feature – some special characteristic, easily highlighted in advertising, which gives the product a special mail order appeal.

How difficult are after-sales problems likely to be?

Whatever the product, a certain percentage of what you sell will be returned to you for refund under the well established mail order practice that if the customer for any reason is not completely happy with his purchase, he can return it and get his money back. This is *not* an after-sales problem; it is simply a feature of mail order trading and you will have to live with it. The only way of keeping such returns to a minimum is to ensure that your advertising gives the customer a fair and unexaggerated idea of the product and that its quality is adequate; by this means you at least avoid returns due to simple disappointment – but see also pages 162–163.

Real after-sales problems arise from product failures within, normally, the first year after purchase, though the guarantee period that you and/or the manufacturer give may be more or less than a year, depending upon the nature of the product and the practice of the trade. Anything that has working parts is unavoidably subject to breakdown; anything that has a function can malfunction. Not only can the electric drill seize up or the kitchen mincer jam, but the hot water bottle can leak and the tines of the garden fork snap. Every time a faulty product is returned to you for refund, replacement or repair, you have an after-sales problem which eats into your profits to a greater or lesser extent. Well made products cause fewer problems than badly made ones; non-mechanical products cause fewer problems than mechanical ones.

You must anticipate after-sales problems and decide, before committing yourself to a product, how you would cope with them and what it would cost you to do so. Have you the skill, equipment, space and time to deal with repairs on your own premises? Does the manufacturer offer a good after-sales service? What extra costs will you incur in parts, postage, packing etc if goods prove faulty? What percentage of faulty items could you tolerate before the entire mail order operation became unprofitable. Don't ever assume that after-sales problems will not occur;

the perfect product has yet to be manufactured. Your task in choosing a product is to strike the right balance between the initial cost of expensive and reliable products and the cost of dealing with the breakdowns of cheaper but less reliable ones.

Are there attractive follow-up possibilities?

What makes initial advertising expensive is that most non-customers aren't going to be interested in your product, and yet you have to pay for the interested and uninterested alike. Once you have gained customers, however, your position changes. The individuals on your list can now be approached directly, and your advertising, previously addressed to the world at large and paid for accordingly, can now be addressed to those already known to you and to whom you are already known. Your direct mail advertising should hit targets much more frequently, and hence your further sales should be acquired at lower cost than your initial ones – always provided, of course, that your later offers appeal to the same sort of people as your earlier ones.

It is therefore important, even when choosing your very first product, to have in mind what further sales you might later be able to make to any customers you now attract. These are the follow-up possibilities, and the long-term success of your business is likely to depend upon them. Make sure that you fully appreciate this: follow-up sales are not bonuses; they are the very heart of your business, and from the start, your efforts must be directed towards securing them.

Suppose you sell a customer some photographic equipment. If you later try to sell lawnmowers or knitting machines, that customer is of little more value to you than a non-customer. In order to exploit your advantage in having a real live customer on your list, you must offer him further products which relate to his known interest.

How successfully your business builds up its proportion of old but active customers to new ones – and therefore its ratio of more profitable customers to less profitable ones – depends in great part on the type of products you sell and the degree of forethought you originally gave to follow-up possibilities.

Consumables

Anything *consumable* – food, drink, stationery supplies, cosmetics, periodical publications, and so on – ought to lead to regular orders from satisfied customers. With such products, you should at best be able to get a customer for life, who reorders, unprompted, at regular intervals. From the mail trader's point of view, this is the main attraction of dealing in consumables: it is, in theory at least, possible to develop a business with a momentum of its own, which, once fully established, needs little conventional advertising at all beyond the enclosure of reorder forms with despatched goods. Of course, even a business successfully established in this way will need to some extent to trawl for new customers to keep the customer list topped up, because some old customers are bound to vanish through loss of interest, changed habits, or simply death, but advertising costs should be minimal. If you can choose a consumable product and market it successfully by mail, you will ultimately have fewer ups and downs than many mail order businesses.

Related items
The principle of choosing a product with an eye to future sales, and not just immediate ones, is important. While consumables have the simplest follow-up possibilities – more of the same – other products, carefully chosen, can also lead on to further sales. Sell someone some running shoes, for example, and he may well later be interested in buying a track suit or books on athletics or a stopwatch, and so on. Your decision as to what to sell today, therefore, must take account of what you are hoping to sell tomorrow.

Developing business expertise
Bear in mind also that it is not only the customer's continuity of interest that is valuable to you. Your own continuity of business practice is also important as it allows you to acquire an expertise in the routines of the purchasing, handling, advertising, packing etc of particular types of product so that over time you develop a specialist's experience and a business organisation that is *in place* to deal in one-off selling campaigns – ski boots this month, lawnmowers the next, and telephone answering machines the month after – you will effectively have business start-up problems over and over again, having to decide for each new product where to advertise, how to advertise, how to store/handle/pack the goods, and so on. Such a business lurches from the frenzied activity of the successes to the depressing calm of the failures, and has little chance of settling into a steadily continuing, well founded enterprise, slowly laying down reserves of goodwill over the years.

Still looking for ideas?

In Appendix 1, a number of products are considered in the light of the comments made in this chapter. You might find it useful both as an illustration of the suggested ways of assessing products for mail order, and possibly also as a prompt to your own thinking in your search for a product.

Chapter 4

Business Basics

If you're going into the mail order business you'll need to know not only about the specifics of mail order but also about the generalities of business. While the rest of the book is about the specifics – things of particular concern to mail order – this chapter is about the generalities that concern all businesses, mail order or otherwise. They include such topics as taxation, professional advice, legal status, staff, premises, raising finance and so on.

If you are already experienced in business or knowledgeable about it, you may safely skip this chapter. Although written with the mail order trader in mind, it is not about specifically mail order matters.

Starting in business

It is quite possible to start a mail order business without any formality whatever. You don't have to ask anyone's permission. If you want to sell clothes or books or watches or computers or most other things by post, all you have to do is to publicise your offer – and you're in business. To sell products like these by mail, you don't need any sort of licence, formal registration or legal documentation. You're in business if you say you're in business, and that's that.

Well, almost that. Some businesses and some business activities do indeed have to be licensed, registered, or in some other way authorised. It's all a question of what you trade in, where you trade from, the manner in which you trade, the terms of trade you offer to your customers, and the volume of trade you expect.

If you sell wines, spirits or tobacco, for example, you will need a licence. If you use your car in connection with your business, you will need your insurers' approval. If you run your business from rented premises, you will need your landlord's consent, and even if you run it from freehold premises, you may need planning permission from the local authority; check the lease or deeds of your property. If you offer certain credit facilities to your customers, you will need a consumer credit licence. If you keep a computerised file of customers' names and addresses, you must register under the Data Protection Act. If your expected turnover exceeds a certain figure, you will have to register as a VAT trader.

And that's just a random selection of the rules and regulations which might affect you.

So this is the problem: how can you be sure that your business activities do not contravene this rule or that regulation? This book will give you an idea of some of the things you should be thinking about, but there is only one sure way of getting a reliable answer to the problem, and that is to take professional advice.

Time spent on background reading is by no means wasted, as this is the easiest way of learning to identify those things you can safely tackle yourself and those for which you need professional help. It is also the easiest way of familiarising yourself with the matters the professionals will be talking to you about and some of the jargon they will be using. This will help you to discuss your business plans intelligently with them, and possibly help you to prompt *their* thinking in the right direction by asking pertinent questions.

Professional advisers

For the business person, there are three indispensable professional advisers: bank manager, accountant, solicitor. Other professionals may also be needed from time to time – surveyors or insurance brokers, for instance – but one or other of your basic trio will be able to refer you to any other professional you might need.

Personal recommendation of this kind is the best way of getting a new professional adviser. Your existing adviser, knowing you and your circumstances, is well placed to recommend other suitable people to you. Furthermore, such a recommendation gives you a convenient introduction to the new person – 'I have been given your name by my accountant, Mr X' – and this goes some way to getting you a more sympathetic consideration than if you had made a cold approach to someone whose name you had picked out of Yellow Pages. From the professional's point of view it makes good sense to be helpful to a client recommended by a colleague, even if there seems to be no immediate likelihood of earning vast fees. Provided no unfavourable report goes back to the recommender, he can always hope that the next client referred to him will be worth a fortune.

So if you are not already fully equipped with the basic trio of advisers but you do have one or two of them, seek a recommendation to whichever of the three you are missing. If at present you have no professional advisers, then get one as soon as possible. A recommendation from a knowledgeable business friend may point you in the right direction. Failing that, get yourself started by opening a business account at a local bank.

The manager of a small branch will probably take more interest in you and your affairs than the manager of a large one. On the other hand, it is normally the case that the larger the branch, the more discretion the manager has to act on his own authority without reference to head office. If you get on well with your bank manager, the one in the larger branch will sometimes be able to help you out financially with less fuss and formality than the one in the smaller branch. However, at this early stage in your business plans, don't agonise too deeply over future imponderables. The important thing is to get started. You can always move your account later.

Once you have opened a bank account, discuss your business plans with the manager, and ask him to recommend a suitable accountant and solicitor to you.

It is important to establish a working relationship with your professional advisers at an early date, so that you can discuss things with them as your plans are forming and turn to them quickly if the need arises. Often enough, a brief telephone call can dispose of a problem that might otherwise become a nagging worry.

Bank manager

Most of the time it is the services of the bank rather than those of the bank manager himself that you use. From your business bank account you make payments to suppliers, and into it you pay money received from customers. Even if you already have a personal bank account, open a separate account for your business so that you, your accountant, and ultimately the taxman, can clearly distinguish between business transactions and personal ones.

The bank manager can advise you on a whole range of business matters, but the primary business of a bank is to lend money. Whenever your business requires more money that it has in hand or than you can provide from your own savings, the bank manager is the person to approach for help. He will, however, expect you to present him with a well argued case, showing precisely the sums you need, why you need them, when you need them, and how and when you expect to be able to pay the interest and repay the capital. All of these things can be shown on a *cash flow forecast*, which gives a detailed breakdown of planned business expenditure month by month for, say, the next half year, together with a prediction of the expected business income month by month over the same period. Your accountant will help you in the preparation of the cash flow forecast.

There's one fundamental respect in which the bank manager differs from your other professional advisers. The others offer only knowledge and expertise, while the bank manager additionally offers – potentially, at any rate – finance, The giving of advice leaves the giver not one whit less secure, but the lending of money puts the lender on risk. As a result, while you, your accountant and solicitor are always in a sense sitting on the same side of the table, your bank manager may be sitting beside you at one moment, and fixing you with a firm eye from across the room the next. The bank's interests and yours will not always be the same; guess who comes off worse when they differ. If you want a chum to stand by you when the going gets tough, read on.

Accountant

The accountant is the professional adviser you will have most dealings with. You consult the others as particular needs arise, but you deal with the accountant on a continuing basis throughout the life of your business. He will help you to set it up in the first place, advise you on bookkeeping, help you monitor the fortunes of the business, prepare annual accounts, and deal on your behalf with the tax authorities. The concern of the accountant is anything to do with business money, and that just about covers everything. Whether you're wondering about forming a limited company, or raising finance, or disputing a tax coding, or are just getting into a muddle with the bookkeeping, pick up the phone and talk to your accountant.

Solicitor

The solicitor's province is the law: licences, leases, local authority permission, contracts and other legal documentation are all the concern of the solicitor. You need to talk things over with him well before committing yourself to your business venture so that he can advise you on the legal requirements and constraints, and, if necessary, help you to apply for any licences or authorisations you may need. If you are planning to buy or rent property, form a partnership, employ staff, sue for non-payment of debts or the non-supply of pre-paid goods your solicitor's the person to see.

The legal status of your business

When you have your first meeting with your first professional adviser, he will probably ask if you have yet decided whether to operate your new mail order business as a sole trader, a limited company or a partnership. While each of these affects the legal status of your business in its dealing with the rest of the world, the pros and cons of each are largely financial, and your accountant is the best person to discuss them with in the first place. The main considerations are set out below.

Sole trader

A sole trader is an individual in business on his own account. The term is slightly misleading in that the sole trader can if he wishes employ any number of staff without affecting his sole trader status. The essential characteristic of the sole trader enterprise is that the proprietor and his business are one and the same in law. Even if Joe Smith trades under such a name as 'Mail Order Marvels', the business name, as far as the law is concerned, is just another name for Joe Smith. Indeed Joe Smith's bank will give him a cheque book showing the account holder as 'JOE SMITH trading as MAIL ORDER MARVELS'.

The major advantage of operating as a sole trader is its simplicity. You can start your business with no legal formalities or fees, and you can implement any business decisions you make without reference to anyone else. You can trade under your own name or a business name, and in neither case is any kind of registration or prior permission required, although if you use a business name, you are additionally required to show your true name on your business stationery and in your advertising.

The major disadvantage of operating as a sole trader is that you are liable for the debts of your business to the full extent of your personal wealth. Your business may get into difficulties through no fault of your own: perhaps there is a postal strike just at the time you have launched an expensive advertising campaign; or perhaps a supplier, whom you had to pay in advance as a new trader, goes bust before supplying you with anything. Whatever the reason for your business difficulties, the people to whom your business owes money can insist that you personally pay them in full, even if this means that you have to sell your car, your furniture or your home to do so.

Tax and the sole trader

Although the law considers the proprietor and his business to be one and the same, the taxman fortunately recognises that a business is a significantly different activity from one's personal life, and he applies a whole set of special rules to it. In the jargon, he will tax you under *Case 1 of Schedule D* for the self-employed rather than under *Schedule E* for those working for someone else. Schedule D allows you to claim as pre-tax expenses considerably more than an employer can claim under Schedule E. Furthermore, whereas an employee's tax is deducted from his pay before he gets it, the self-employed person's tax does not become due for payment until many months after the profits it is based upon have been in the trader's hands.

What do you pay tax on?
Not all money coming into the business can be regarded as profit, and it's only profit that is taxable. Your customers may in a given year send you £30,000 in cheques and postal orders for the things you sell by mail, but if during the same year you spend £10,000 on advertising, £5000 on buying goods for resale, and a further £3000 on sundry business expenses, then your profits clearly amount to only £12,000, and this is the sum on which you will be taxed.

When is the tax levied and paid?
Setting your allowable business expenses against your total income to arrive at your taxable profit – if you've made any – is something the taxman requires you to do only once a year. And it may be several months into the following year before you and your accountant are able to finalise the figures.

In recognition of this, the taxman normally assesses your tax on what is known as the *preceding year basis*. This means that the tax you pay *this* year is based upon the profit or loss you made *last* year. The situation is complicated by the fact that whereas a year for most ordinary mortals is thought to run from 1 January to 31 December, the taxman's year runs from 6 April to 5 April, and your business year can be any 12-month period you choose, provided only that having made your choice, you stick to it.

Suppose your business year, normally referred to as your *accounting year*, runs from 1 July to 30 June. For the tax year 6 April 1992 to 5 April 1993, you will pay tax on the profit or loss your business made in the accounting year which ended in the previous tax year. The previous tax year ended, of course, on 5 April 1992, and your accounting year which ended in that tax year ran from 1 July 1990 to 30 June 1991, so that is the business period on which you are assessed for tax in the 1992–93 tax year. Try reading that again slowly.

Schedule D tax is due for payment in two equal instalments: half on 1 January in the year of assessment and half on the following 1 July.

You can see that there is a considerable delay between the period which generates the tax liability and the time the tax is actually paid. In the example, taxable income started to accrue at 1 July 1990 but the tax liability is not finally discharged until 1 July 1993. This does not mean, of course, that you get any kind of 'tax holiday': your business is taxed in full from day one onwards. What it does mean is that your tax *payments* are always made in arrears.

Your accountant will help you choose an accounting year which, consistent with your other needs, will maximise the delay between earning profits and paying tax on them. Don't be surprised if it turns out that your first accounting year runs for less than or more than 12 months; that's all allowed for in the complications of the fiscal rules which keep so many taxmen and accountants gainfully employed.

If, by the way, you make a loss in any year, there will of course be no tax to pay, and the loss itself can be set off against other sources of income for that year or carried forward to be set against the profits of future years.

Special rules for new sole traders
In the first three years of business, special rules apply. Plainly, in your first business year there is no preceding year upon which a tax assessment can be made; so for this year you are taxed on your actual profits during the tax year. In your second year, you are taxed upon the profits made in your first 12 months of trading, which will necessarily include the same opening months which were assessed for tax in your first year. In your third year, you switch to the preceding year basis, paying tax on profits made in your preceding accounting year, and you continue on this basis for the life of the business.

The effect of these special rules is that your first three tax assessments are all based upon your earliest months of trading. This is likely to be to your advantage if, like most businesses, your profits are lowest in the early days and improve over time. If it turns out that the special rules do not work to your advantage, you can elect to be taxed on your actual tax-year profits in your first three years.

There are further rules which allow you to set business losses in your first four tax years against non-business income in the three years before you started the business.

Whew!
If all of this seems impossibly confusing, take heart, your accountant will sort it all out for you; you just have to pay the tax bills when he tells you to. You would be wise, however, to set aside money for tax as you go along so that when the bill does eventually arrive, you will be able to pay it without embarrassment. Earmark for the taxman a third of any money you draw from the business for personal use, and you won't go far wrong.

Once your accountant and the taxman have agreed on your business profit for any year – allowing for any offsetting losses from earlier years – the tax you pay on it is exactly the same as the tax you would have paid if you had earned the same amount as an employee on somebody's else's payroll.

National Insurance (NI) and the sole trader

A sole trader has to pay Class 2 National Insurance contributions (NIC), and possibly Class 4 as well. Class 2 is a flat rate of £5.35 a week, while Class 4 is 6.3 per cent of profits falling between £6120 and £21,060 a year (1992 – 93 rates). Note that the sole trader does not qualify for the full range of NI benefits; in particular, he is not eligible for unemployment benefit, sick pay or the earnings-related part of the state pension, despite the fact that his Class 4 NIC is also earnings-related.

NIC rates are normally changed each year. Up-to-date information may be found in the DSS leaflet NI.208, obtainable from your local social security office.

Limited company

A limited company is a legal entity in its own right, responsible for its own debts. The shareholders' liability for the company's debts is limited to the extent of the money they have already paid, or undertaken to pay, for their shares, hence the 'limited' in 'limited company'. If commercial disaster befalls the company because of a defaulting supplier, or a strike in the postal services, or for any other reason, the company may be forced to cease trading, sell off such assets as it has to the highest bidder, and use the proceeds to pay off its creditors as far as it can. If there is not enough money to meet all the outstanding debts, then those debts remain to that extent unpaid. There is no question of the shareholders being called upon to meet the company's debts from their own personal resources; nor – assuming that they have behaved fraudulently – do the directors of the company have any financial liability, unless they have voluntarily entered into some separate agreement to underwrite the company's debts.

The latter position can arise when a company without worthwhile assets borrows money for investment or working capital. The bank or other lender in such a case often requires private security for the loan. The director of a new company borrowing money may thus find that he has to give his personal guarantee as a private individual to repay the loan if the company should be unable to do so. His personal wealth, therefore, is at risk in precisely the same way as it would be if he were operating as a sole trader. Note, however, that this only applies when a personal guarantee is specifically given in connection with a specific transaction; in all other cases the limited liability rules apply.

Although a minimum of two people are needed to form a company, this should present you with no problem even if you intend to run the business effectively as a one-person enterprise. The second person need not take an active part in the business. Your accountant will form a company for you and will deal with all such seeming difficulties as this. So operating as a limited company is a direct alternative to operating as a sole trader, no matter how large or small your mail order venture.

Setting up and running a limited company, however, is more complicated than going into business as a sole trader. You will have professional fees in the setting up of the business, additional accountancy fees once it is trading, as your accounts have to be *audited* (ie checked and verified by a suitably qualified person, probably your accountant), and an annual fee of £32 to lodge those accounts each year with the Registrar of Companies. Your accountant will explain to you the various other obligations you are under as a company director.

Tax and the limited company

Because a limited company is a legal entity, it is subject to tax in its own right. This is *corporation tax*, the tax the company has to pay on any profits retained within the company. Those profits not retained, but paid out to directors and other employees as salaries or to shareholders as dividends, are taxed as income in the hands of the recipients.

The rate of corporation tax for company profits up to £250,000 is normally the same as the basic rate of income tax for individuals – 25 per cent in 1992–93. The tax is due for payment nine months after the end of the company's accounting year.

If a company makes a loss in any given year, it has of course no tax to pay; and the loss can be carried forward to offset profits in future years. A company cannot, however, offset its losses against any other income of its directors, and in this respect, particularly in the early years, it is at a disadvantage compared to the sole trader enterprise.

The company director

The taxman considers a director to be an employee of the company. So even though you may own 99 per cent of the company's shares, and feel in every respect just as self-employed as the sole trader, the taxman considers you to be a company employee, subject to tax under Schedule E. As a result, even if yours is effectively a one-person business, the company has to operate the pay-as-you-earn (PAYE) system, accounting month by month to the taxman for any tax and NIC that are due in respect of your salary.

National Insurance, the company and the director

As an employee of the company, you have to pay Class 1 NIC on any income between £2808 and £21,060; the rate varies from 2 per cent of pay at the lower limit to 9 per cent of pay at the top. (These figures and those below are 1992-93 rates.)

However, not only are you employed by the company, the company also employs you. That may sound like the same thing said in two different ways, but it nevertheless gives rise to two lots of NIC. In addition to the NIC which you pay as an employee, there is a further NIC which your company has to pay as your employer. The latter NIC is payable on any salary over £2808, and the rate varies from 4.6 per cent at the lower limit to 10.4 per cent on a salary over £9880. Note that for the company's NIC – unlike the employee's NIC – there is no upper limit to the salary on which contributions are payable.

No NIC is payable in respect of dividends or retained profits.

Tax efficiency

The different tax and NI treatment of company profits, dividends and salaries, gives your accountant a chance to earn his keep for you by retaining or distributing profits in the most tax-efficient manner. With a limited company your tax affairs will be more complicated but also more flexible than those of the sole trader.

Partnership

A partnership can be as simple to set up as a sole trader enterprise. Two or more people can decide to go into the mail order business together, and if they do, then they're in business, and that's that. There are no legal formalities that they are obliged to go through. However, while business partnerships can come into being very simply, terminating them or adjusting them – perhaps because a partner dies or wishes to leave the business – can be a nightmare.

Suppose three people pool their savings, call themselves 'Shirts by Post', buy a warehouse, fill it from top to bottom with shirts, and then launch a mail order advertising campaign. What happens if one of the three decides shortly afterwards that he wants to pull out of the business, and insists on taking with him the money he originally put into it? You can't sell off a third of a warehouse or instantly turn a third of your stock into cash; you can't sell off a third of the partnership's van or of its computerised stock-control system. Perhaps the remaining partners could buy out the third partner's share, but what if they don't want to or haven't got the money? One way or another, the business is at risk and at the very least will be fundamentally changed.

If the partners had instead formed themselves into a limited company, the problem would not have arisen. As shareholders in the company, any one of them would be free to leave and sell his shareholding if he wished, but he could not insist that the company's assets be sold off so that he could recover his original investment. The limited company would continue in existence even if all three of the founders sold off their shares.

There are other problems with partnerships, most of them deriving from the sad truth that human beings, however enthusiastic they are to cooperate during the heady days of optimistic planning, frequently fall to disputing about this and that once the plans have to be implemented and some of the hopes have perhaps started to turn a little sour.

The main disadvantage of a partnership is that, just like the sole trader, the partners have unlimited personal liability for the debts of the business. Furthermore, this liability falls not merely upon each of them individually but also upon the partnership as a whole. If a partnership of three people, for example, incurs debts which the business itself cannot meet, the partners can be legally forced to pay off those debts from their personal wealth – even if, as with the sole trader, this means selling off everything, including one's home. Worse still, if it should turn out that, say, two of the partners have no personal wealth, the third partner is legally bound to meet the full debts of the partnership himself.

Some of the inherent disadvantages of the partnership set-up can be avoided by a formally drawn-up Deed of Partnership. For this, you will need to consult your solicitor and it will, of course, give rise to legal fees. A formal deed of this kind can do much to regulate the internal affairs of a partnership, and is very strongly to be recommended if you are thinking of running your mail order business as a partnership. What such a deed cannot do is in any way limit the liabilities of the partners and the partnership to the world at large. The only way to get limited liability is to form a limited company.

Tax, NIC and the partnership

For tax and NI purposes, the individual members of a partnership are treated as sole traders with respect to their share of the partnership's profits.

Value Added Tax (VAT)

If your business turnover exceeds or over the next thirty days is expected to exceed £36,600 a year, you will have to register as a VAT trader (1992–93 figures). The threshold figure is normally increased in line with inflation year by year. Your local VAT office (look under 'Customs & Excise' in the phone book) will tell you the current figure, and supply you with all the information you need if you are required to register.

Note that the obligation to register depends solely upon *turnover*; it has nothing to do with profit. Your next door neighbour may make a comfortable living as an investment consultant, with profits of perhaps £30,000 on a turnover of £35,000: he does not have to register for VAT. You, on the other hand, may be expecting profits of no more than £15,000 on a mail order turnover of £90,000: you *do* have to register for VAT.

If you are a sole trader, all your business activities, assuming there are others in addition to your mail order ones, are lumped together for the purposes of VAT liability. A partnership or a limited company are registered for VAT as a partnership or as a limited company, no account being taken of any other business activity of the partners or directors.

As a VAT trader you have to collect VAT from your customers – this is your *output tax* but you can also claim back from the VAT man any tax that your business has had to pay to its suppliers – this is your *input tax*. At quarterly intervals you draw up a VAT account of your outputs and inputs, and send the VAT man a cheque for the difference if your output tax is greater or claim a refund from him if your input tax is greater.

Most products and services, both of which are referred to in VAT jargon as *supplies*, are subject to VAT at the standard rate; this is currently (1992) 17.5 per cent, but could of course be changed by the government at any time. A few supplies – books and children's clothing, for example – are *zero-rated*; this means that the trader has no output tax to collect but can still claim a refund on any input tax. Some supplies are *exempt* – insurance brokerage, for example – and the consequence for the trader is that no output tax has to be collected, but neither can any input tax be reclaimed.

Raising finance

It is not easy for a business beginner to raise finance. Most lenders prefer to see a track record rather than just an optimistic plan before they part with their money. At the very least, they expect you to put up a substantial part of the total requirement yourself. So your first task is to work out how much you can provide from your own resources, and whether this comes anywhere near your total needs. Take your accountant's advice on whether you can be seriously in the market for the kind of loan you need; and if your plans look too grandiose for your pocket, cut them down to size. It is better to start small than not to start at all. It is also better not to over-extend yourself, borrowing every last penny you can and leaving yourself no margin for unforeseen difficulties.

While borrowing from relatives and friends may look an attractive possibility, especially as they may well not charge you a commercial rate of interest, avoid it if you can. Business is always a risk. Things can and do go wrong. Why put family and friendship in jeopardy if there are commercial lenders you can approach whose very business is risk-taking?

A rather better idea would be to go into partnership or form a company with other people who have some money. But then, of course, the business and its direction would no longer be exclusively in your hands, and its ultimate profits would not go exclusively into your pocket. But it is well worth considering joining forces with other people if they can not only bring money into the business but also useful skills and knowledge, particularly in those areas where your own skills and knowledge are wanting.

But suppose you have concluded that you have adequate money of your own to invest, and that it is reasonable for you to look for further funding from outside. How do you go about it?

Long-term and short-term finance

You should first of all have a clear understanding of the kind of finance you need. For investment in such things as property, plant and equipment, you need long-term finance. For help with meeting the business's day-to-day debts you need short-term finance.

Suppose you need £30,000 to buy the freehold of combined warehouse and office premises, but can put up only £10,000 yourself. You and your accountant put your heads together, consider the revenue from your proposed mail order venture, and calculate that the business should generate enough profit to pay off a £20,000 loan – capital and interest – over, say, 10 years. The need, plainly, is for long-term money which the lender guarantees not to call in ahead of time provided you make the agreed repayments, because if he did call in the loan, you might have no option but to sell up in order to release the value locked up in the bricks and mortar of the property. A forced sale of this kind could put an end to your business altogether.

You may also need to spend, say, £50,000 on stock. You hope, however, that within two or three months of purchasing the stock you will have sold it all at a comfortable profit. The problem is that there may be a delay between the time when your suppliers require payment and the time when money starts coming in from your customers. So you may need as much as £50,000 to cover this interim period. Furthermore, even when the stock is sold and you are in funds again, you will of course want to make other stock purchases for other mail order campaigns, and you are likely once again to find yourself temporarily strapped for cash. Indeed your cash position could oscillate like this indefinitely: fairly short periods when you're flush with funds alternating with fairly short periods when you haven't enough in hand to pay the bills. Although, therefore, you have a regular need for financial help, it is needed only temporarily and for a short period each time. Plainly, your requirement is for short-term money.

Fixed-term loans v overdrafts
Long-term money is best covered by fixed-term loans which the lender is unable to cancel unless you default on your repayments. Short-term money is most cheaply covered by an overdraft facility at the bank.

An *overdraft facility* permits you to spend up to an agreed amount more than you have in your account at any given time, the bank charging you interest only on the amount and for the days that you are overdrawn. The facility is very simple and flexible to operate, and once arranged can be used up to the agreed limit without seeking the bank's permission every time you risk going into the red. While an overdraft facility is normally cheaper and more flexible than a fixed-term loan, the flexibility cuts both ways: the bank can withdraw the facility at any time.

Sources of finance
Whatever type of finance you require, the bank is your likeliest source of funds, and your accountant the best person to help you prepare a cash flow forecast (see page 55) to support your case and give the lender the confidence to put his money at risk.

If your own bank won't help you, try other banks. If none of the banks will help, try other lenders; take your accountant's advice on this or even your bank manager's – he may know of other suitable sources of finance even if he is not prepared to lend money himself.

Hire purchase and leasing
If you're short of money for fixed assets like plant or equipment, consider the possibility of hire purchase or leasing. Both methods allow you to make regular payments instead of having to find one large lump sum; they differ, however, in that under a hire purchase agreement you eventually become the owner of the goods, while under a leasing agreement you never do.

Help from the state
There are a number of sources of government, local government and institutional finance and assistance for new and small businesses. Enterprise Allowance schemes have already been mentioned (page 12), but other sources of finance are available at different times, different places, for different types of people and for different types of business venture. No single published source gathers together all this information, and it is anyway subject to change over quite short periods of time.

Undoubtedly the best way to inform yourself of what is currently available is to call on one or more of the high street banks – they often have readily available literature for business beginners, some of it providing further contact names and addresses which may be relevant to your own circumstances and ambitions. When your business plans are beginning to take on a positive shape, a preliminary interview with the bank manager will also be helpful. A similar meeting with your accountant and with someone at the local Jobcentre may yield useful information as well. Most approaches of this kind generally produce a suggested approach to another source, and while you may sometimes feel you are on a wild goose chase, every avenue is worth exploring because without adequate finance your business will either never get started or will come to a premature end.

Good housekeeping keeps the bills down
Just as you can find two families with similar budgets, one of whom runs a comfortable home with all the family well fed and clothed, while the other is constantly getting into debt and running out of basic necessities, so you can find business people who are good financial managers and others who are not. Make sure you're in the former category, and this alone will reduce your dependence on outside finance.

Take the maximum credit your suppliers will allow you. Chase up your own debtors promptly. Don't waste money on non-revenue-producing luxuries: most mail order businesses, for example, can run as effectively out of grotty warehouse premises on the wrong side of town as they can from 'prestige' addresses that make your notepaper a joy to look at. Above all, watch the money day by day; if things start to go wrong, you need to know as soon as possible. Tight financial control is one of the major characteristics of a well run business. And bookkeeping is where it all starts.

Bookkeeping

Money is very simple stuff. Only two things can happen to it as far as your business is concerned: either you give it to someone else or someone else gives it to you. Keeping a record of this two-way traffic is at bottom all that bookkeeping is about.

If you are a registered VAT trader, you are legally obliged to keep the books in such a way that the VAT component of you transactions may be readily identified. A limited company, whether registered for VAT or not, is also obliged to keep accounts. The partners of a partnership will doubtless require that whichever of them is responsible for the paying out and taking in of money keeps a written record of all transactions so that the other partners can always check to see what's going on. The sole trader, if he is not registered for VAT, is under no obligation to do any bookkeeping at all; but he would be exceedingly foolish not to do so since without written records to support his case, he would almost certainly come off worse in any dispute he might have with the Inland Revenue.

In short, no business is too new or too small to keep proper business records. Your accountant will show you what needs to be done and will set up an appropriate bookkeeping system for you. But even before he does so, you would be wise to keep a record of all your preliminary transactions. To start with, a couple of small cashbooks and ringfiles will do, the sort of thing that you can get at any local stationer's. Use one of the cashbooks and one of the ringfiles for money coming in, and the others for money going out. Whenever you receive any money or spend any money, make a cashbook entry; give the transaction a serial number, and then write details of when, what and how much. Your 'Payments Made' book, for example, might start off like this:

1	6.5.92	XYZ Warehouse: stock samples	13.85
2	7.5.92	Copyshop: printed letterheads	47.50
3	7.5.92	Woolworths: paper punch	3.49

The 'Payments Made' ringfile would contain the supporting documents – receipts, invoices, orders etc – which are your evidence that these transactions have taken place; mark each document at the top righthand corner with the identifying cashbook serial number, so that there will be no difficulty in future in matching cashbook entry to supporting document.

Even a bookkeeping system as rudimentary as this is infinitely better than no system at all, and it will enable you with a minimum of fuss and confusion to convert your early records in due course to whatever more permanent and thorough-going system your accountant proposes.

Mail order lends itself to detailed bookkeeping since every transaction, however small, naturally gives rise to its own documentation. The market trader, for example, starts his day with a stall full of goods and ends it with a bag full of money, but has no means of recalling in detail who bought what and for how much. The mail trader, by contrast, necessarily receives a separate document showing customer's name, address, order and payment, for every sale he makes; and of course, like all other business people, he receives separate documentation for each purchase he makes too.

Trade supplies

To find sources of trade supply, consult appropriate trade directories and trade journals. Yellow pages, though not a trade directory, is also an excellent source of information about local trade suppliers.

Your local public library will probably have a general trade directory or two on its reference shelves, and the main reference library of your area will almost certainly have more – and more up-to-date – general directories and possibly some specialised directories as well. General trade directories cover all trades in a particular geographical area, which may be as narrow as a single town or as broad as the whole world. Specialised trade directories deal solely with a particular trade or related group of trades, usually over the whole country, sometimes over the whole world.

Trade journals concern themselves with particular trades or groups of trades. Their advertising and editorial reviews provide the most accessible up-to-date information for anyone entering a particular area of business for the first time.

One of the best ways of discovering which directories and journals cover your own area of business interest is to consult your local public reference librarian. Even if the library itself does not stock the particular publications you require, the librarian has the reference books that enable him to identify suitable titles; if you wish, you can then order these, as appropriate, through your local bookshop or newsagent, or write direct to the publishers. Alternatively, the librarian may be able to refer you to other libraries where the titles which interest you are held in stock.

Once you have found names and addresses of possible suppliers, you then have the problem of getting specific supply information – price, availability, delivery, credit etc – so that you can make your decisions and in due course place an order. The important thing at this stage is to present a businesslike appearance: make sure that you have properly printed business stationery, and if you possibly can, see that any letters you send are well typed. Trade suppliers are often suspicious of newcomers, and may well require references from you and other evidence of your business standing. Don't be surprised or indignant if your bona fides are challenged. Be ready to give trade references if possible, ie suppliers with whom you have already dealt, and be ready to supply, or even to volunteer, the names and addresses of your professional advisers to whom enquiries may be made.

Premises: home or away?

Home

As a way of keeping overheads low in the early experimental stages of the business, the advantage of running it from home has already been mentioned. Further, you may be able to claim a proportion of your domestic running costs – heating, lighting etc – as a pre-tax business expense, though this could have capital gains tax implications if you decide to sell your home in the future. Discuss this with your accountant.

Running a business from home does have snags. In addition to the possible need for permission from a landlord and/or local authority, you may also find that there may be in the deeds of the property restrictive covenants specifically forbidding its use for business purposes. Your solicitor is the person to see in order to check out all of these things. Some of the apparent restrictions, however theoretically severe, may not in practice amount to very much. Many people quietly get on with their businesses until somebody starts screaming, and often enough nobody ever does.

A more likely source of difficulty for home-based mail order businesses is the appearance of customers on the doorstep at all hours. Even if your advertising makes plain that you supply by mail order only, there will always be an irreducible percentage of people who will try to call at your address in person. How much embarrassment this causes you depends upon your other commitments and domestic arrangements.

Perhaps the greatest difficulty is that a home-based business, however thriving, doesn't *look* like a business. You may have problems getting the media to accept your advertising, or trade suppliers to accept your orders.

None of these problems need be permanently disabling, but they may put constraints upon your business practice and development that you would not have if you were operating from conventional business premises.

Away

If you are looking for warehouse and office space, approach those estate agents who have commercial departments and the more specialist business transfer agents. Find names and addresses of both in Yellow Pages. Your local newspaper may also carry advertising of interest to you; if it does, it will help you identify the active agents in your area.

The location of business premises has almost no importance whatsoever for mail order. Even if your premises are decidedly off the beaten track, there should be no adverse effect upon your sales. The public well understands that any mail order business is as near as the nearest pillar-box, and its precise location really doesn't matter, provided only that it is in this country and may be reached by ordinary letter or phone call.

Choose premises which offer you internally the space and facilities you require, and which look convenient enough for suppliers, staff and yourself.

Your finances will determine whether you should prefer freehold or leasehold property. The advantage of freehold property is that it will probably appreciate in value with time, and so may be regarded as an investment in its own right, quite apart from the mail order business you intend to run from it. On the other hand, it will certainly be more costly in the short term than comparable leasehold premises. Yet another of the matters you will need to discuss with your accountant.

Your solicitor too will be much involved with your acquisition of property. If you intend to buy, he will make all the necessary enquiries for you, examining the deeds, checking with the local authority on the permitted uses of the property, asking about any road construction or other building plans that might affect the property, and so on. If you are intending to rent, he will check the terms of the lease, see that your proposed business may lawfully be carried on there, and that you have adequate security of tenure. Whether buying or leasing, consult your solicitor at an early date, and make no commitment until you have discussed things with him. Remember, it is entirely possible for a binding contract to come into existence merely by word of mouth. If you say to a seller, 'This warehouse is just what I'm looking for. I can offer you £20,000 for it', and the seller says to you, 'I accept', then the contract's made, and it will be too late to learn the following day that the council are intending to demolish the property to make way for a new road. By all means express your genuine interest in a property, but leave it to your solicitor to make any offers on your behalf.

Staff

For senior personnel, you might approach agencies who specialise in executive staff. Look up the Yellow Pages covering the nearest large city. For more junior or less important staff, try your local Jobcentre or one of the commercial employment agencies which you will doubtless find in your nearest big town.

As an employer, you will be responsible for deducting income tax and NIC from your employees' pay before handing the balance to them. So as soon as you take on your first employee, tell your local tax office and they will provide you with the documentation and guidance you need. You will also be bound to observe the many employment laws and

71

regulations which cover everything from race discrimination, maternity rights and redundancy to minimum working temperatures, first-aid provision and an adequate supply of drinking water.

As soon as you employ someone, a contract of employment comes into being even if you do not – as you are legally required to – put the terms and conditions of employment in writing. This is plainly a matter for your solicitor, and you should consult him *before* taking on your first member of staff, so that he can draw up for you a suitable contract of employment which will protect your interests as far as possible.

For as long as you, or you and your partners, work alone, you are able to devote your full energy to the main objective: getting and fulfilling mail orders. Once you take on staff, some of your efforts will have to be directed towards staff management and welfare. Don't underestimate the diversion of energy this may entail.

Chapter 5

Mail Order Constraints

In the now happily receding past, the public image of mail order was roughly on a par with that of secondhand car dealing. It seemed a business activity to which the shady and unscrupulous naturally gravitated. No matter that the overwhelming majority of dealers conducted their businesses fairly and honestly, the general image was tarnished by the behaviour of the rogues.

The reason why mail order has improved in public estimation – and is still improving – is not that the number of rogues in the world has diminished, but that when they try to move into mail order, they find the doors barred against them by various consumer protection measures which have been put in place in recent years.

Unfortunately, the same measures that keep out the baddies also put obstacles in the way of the entirely honest newcomer hoping to get into the business, and set limits on what he can do and how he can do it. Some of these mail order constraints are enshrined in the law of the land, while others are of the self-regulatory kind set out in voluntary codes of practice. Even the voluntary codes are not all that voluntary as far as the trader is concerned, because they are supervised and enforced by bodies over whom the individual dealer, especially the small newcomer to the business, has no control, and yet whose approval he needs if his business development is not to be severely curtailed.

In addition to those constraints that specifically related to mail order, there is also a good deal more general consumer protection legislation which the mail trader, along with all others offering goods and services to the general public, needs to be aware of.

The law

You can think of the laws of the land as being of two kinds. There are those that seek to codify standards of behaviour which the ordinary person's innate sense of right and wrong make him observe anyway. And there are those which have an arbitrariness about them, laws which our legislators have decided will be conducive to the public good, even if an ordinary mortal, sitting alone in his room for a hundred years, would never have dreamt of them.

Laws in the former category cause the honest citizen so little difficulty that he need hardly concern himself with their existence at all. If you have a row with the man next door, you don't ring up your solicitor to see if you're allowed to murder him. Nor, if you are a mail order dealer, would you think you needed to seek legal advice to establish whether you can advertise a nylon blouse as *100% pure silk* or a list of a couple of dozen local wholesalers as a *comprehensive guide to UK sources of trade supply*. Such descriptions are clearly downright lies, and you would not, of course, consider promoting your products like this, law or no law.

However, did you know that there are occasions when it is illegal to describe your product as, for example, *only half the manufacturer's recommended price* even if it *is* only half the manufacturer's recommended price? Or that you may be guilty of an offence if you offer to allow your customers to settle up for their purchases in, say, five instalments rather than by a single payment, even if the five instalments together exactly equal the single payment with no interest added?

Laws in this latter category can cause the most upright trader to stumble, merely out of ignorance, which itself will be no defence if he ever finds himself in the dock.

Below are some of the main points to bear in mind if you are to avoid trouble with the law. As always, if you are unclear about your legal position on any matter, consult your solicitor.

Trade descriptions

Any description you apply to your product must be true. This applies not merely to verbal descriptions, as in the nylon/silk example above, but also to implied descriptions in the illustrations in your advertising and sales literature. If, for example, your ad for an electric drill includes a picture of someone apparently using it to penetrate a concrete floor whereas in truth the drill is incapable of doing any such thing, then you will be as guilty of applying a false trade description as if you had told the lie in plain English.

The relevant legislation is contained in the Trade Descriptions Acts 1968 and 1972.

Price claims

Particularly important trade descriptions are your price claims. For most products, you are permitted to point out that your price differs by a certain amount from the manufacturer's recommended price. But it is illegal to make such a claim, however true, for certain specified products; these include, for example, various floor coverings, electric domestic appliances and indoor furniture. Check the current legal position for your own type of product with the Office of Fair Trading, your solicitor or your specific trade association (see page 95).

Another price claim you should make only with the greatest care concerns your current price in relation to one you formerly charged. If you say, for example, *We've slashed our price by £5!*, it is not enough that the claim is true; it must also be the case that you have offered the goods at the higher price for at least 28 consecutive days in the last six months, and furthermore, that you have indeed sold, not merely offered, the product at that price.

Quality

Any goods you sell must be of *merchantable quality* – that is, fit for the purpose for which they are sold. An article's fitness for its purpose is basically a matter of common sense. An alarm clock that doesn't ring or a freezer incapable of turning water into ice are clearly not fit for their purpose.

But your responsibility as a retailer may go further than this if your customer specifically relies upon your expertise. Suppose you are advertising a number of different adhesives, and a customer, instead of ordering one of them by name, writes to ask for something suitable to mend a broken china teapot. If the adhesive you supply fails to do the job, then the product you supplied was not fit for the purpose, and your customer has a legitimate complaint against you.

Note that the legal responsibility for the merchantable quality of the goods you sell is *yours*; it is not a responsibility you can duck by referring a dissatisfied customer to the manufacturer. The mail order transaction is legally a contract between you and your customer; and if your product is not of merchantable quality, your customer will legitimately look to you for redress. You may in your turn complain to the manufacturer, but that is an entirely separate matter.

The relevant legislation is the Sale of Goods Act 1979.

Credit

You will possibly need a licence if you wish to supply goods on credit. The licensing authority is the Office of Fair Trading, to whom application should be made in advance of your seeking to trade in this way.

The reason why a licence is merely a *possible* requirement for credit traders is that there are some forms of mail order dealing which, while credit sales in plain English, nevertheless fall outside the provisions of the relevant act – the Consumer Credit Act 1974.

You do not require a licence if you merely supply something in advance of payment, which the customer then settles in not more than four instalments. Nor do you need a licence if you allow your customers to pay for their purchases, say, once a month when you render them a statement of account: but this exemption only applies if customers settle their accounts *in full by a single payment* in each accounting period.

The commonest exempt credit activity in mail order is accepting the credit cards issued by other companies – Barclaycard or Access, for example. While the credit card companies themselves need to be licensed, the individual trader does not.

On the other hand, you do need to be licensed if you introduce customers to other suppliers of credit, even if you do not give the credit yourself. You may sell expensive cameras, for example, and have an arrangement with a hire purchase company to whom you refer your customers. Although the company pays you in full and then collects payment in instalments direct from the customer, so that you are in no way giving credit yourself, this counts as a *credit brokerage* activity on your part, and you will accordingly need a licence.

If your credit sales do bring you within the scope of the Act, you must further ensure that the advertising and implementation of your credit terms conform to the requirement of the Act. You will receive details if your licence application is accepted. Fortunately, most readers of this book will not find themselves needing a licence at all.

Data protection

You are required to register as a *data user* under the Data Protection Act 1984 if you hold personal data on a computer file. The names and addresses of living people count as personal data. Every mail order business is bound to have a file of customers and/or enquirers, and the only question you need consider, therefore, is how the information is stored. You don't have to register, no matter how extensive or detailed your records, unless the information is held on a computer. If it *is* held on a computer, even a list of a dozen names copied straight off the electoral roll will oblige you to register. The current (1992) registration fee is £75.

The effect of registration is to give you a legal right to hold personal data on a computer file, but it also imposes upon you certain legal obligations. These include not only the commercially prudent ones of keeping the list accurate, up-to-date, and available only to authorised users, but also such obligations as allowing a customer access to his own record so that he can check its accuracy. Quite what happens if he then objects to seeing himself signalled as, for example, a slow payer, is uncertain. Will there be lengthy disputes as to what precisely constitutes slowness of payment?

Note that registration under the Act is no mere formality like buying a TV licence. The Registrar has the power to refuse an application, or to deregister a data user who breaks the rules. Anyone in breach of the Act may be taken to court; and there are some offences established by the Act which may lead, on conviction, to unlimited fines.

Your published name and address
If you invite customers to send money in advance of the despatch of goods – *selling off the page* is how press ads of this kind are described – your advertising must include your true name and the full address at which the business is managed. This is the requirement of the Mail Order Transactions (Information) Order 1976, an order made under the provisions of the Fair Trading Act 1973. The true name of an individual is his surname, with or without first names or initials; the true name of a limited company is its corporate name.

The Order does not prevent you from using a business name, but whether you do or not, your real name must be clearly shown in your advertising. Similarly, you can if you wish use a PO Box address, but whether you do or not, a full postal address must be clearly shown.

These legal requirements apply to *any* communication which asks for cash in advance. If you first invite people to write in for details, for example, with a view to sending them full sales information in reply – a procedure known as *two-stage selling* – it would be acceptable for your press ad to say *Get your free catalogue from Mailman, PO Box 99, London N23.* But you would need to include your real name and full address in the reply you mail to enquirers if that reply contains an invitation (express or implied) to send a pre-paid order by post.

Business advertisements
The Business Advertisements (Disclosure) Order 1977 requires that anyone advertising goods for sale by way of trade should ensure that the advertisement is plainly a trade advertisement and cannot be mistaken for a private one. This too is an order under the Fair Trading Act 1973.

Anything else?
There are various legal requirements which relate to products of particular types. Such requirements are not specifically directed at the mail trader, but must of course be obeyed by him along with everyone else. To check whether there is any legislation particularly affecting your own product, you should, as ever, consult your solicitor. The Office of Fair Trading or your trade association may also be able to advise you.

If you want to look at the precise wording of a particular piece of legislation yourself, you can buy copies of any of the Acts and Orders mentioned above, or any other statute, from Her Majesty's Stationery Office.

Voluntary codes of practice and consumer protection schemes

Strangely enough, you are likely as a new mail trader to feel less affected by the law than by the voluntary codes and schemes. This is because the guardians of the law normally take no interest in what you're doing until you do something wrong. On the other hand, the self-regulatory bodies may take the most detailed interest in you and your business before you get the chance to do anything at all.

Advertisements and advertising are what self-regulation is mainly concerned with, and the mail trader needs to be familiar with those codes and schemes affecting both advertising in general and mail order advertising in particular.

The British Code of Advertising Practice (BCAP)

BCAP sets out the rules which those involved in advertising have agreed to follow in order to ensure that advertisements can be trusted. The preparation, amendment and observance of *BCAP* is the responsibility of the CAP under the supervision of the ASA (see page 32).

BCAP lies at the heart of the advertising world's self-regulation, and it is frequently taken as the starting point for other more specific codes and schemes. In addition to its well known slogan that *All advertisements should be legal, decent, honest and truthful*, it also gives detailed guidelines on what is acceptable in ads for everything from health cures to betting systems. Although conformity to *BCAP* will not guarantee the acceptability of your advertising to the media, failure to conform will almost certainly result in its rejection.

Section C.VI of *BCAP* specifically concerns mail order advertising. It stresses the need for goods to conform to accepted standards, eg a British Standard if one exists, and to conform to their advertised descriptions. It gives guidelines on acceptable practices in the supply of goods on approval, the refunding of pre-payments when a customer returns unwanted goods, and the time within which all orders should be fulfilled: not more than 28 days except in such special cases as made-to-measure goods.

Copies of *BCAP* are available from the ASA.

British Code of Sales Promotion Practice (BCSPP)

Like *BCAP* above, *BCSPP* is a code under the auspices of the ASA. It deals with such promotional devices as premium offers, reduced price and free offers, the distribution of vouchers, coupons and samples, personality promotions, charity-linked promotions, and prize promotions of all types. If you find yourself concerned with any of these things, get a copy of *BCSPP* from the ASA.

Mail Order Protection Schemes (MOPS)

The central activity that MOPS are concerned with is off-the-page selling. For both the beginner and the established trader, this is one of the most appealing forms of mail order since, in theory at least, you can get your sales message very quickly to millions of people, and the day after can start getting in all those lovely cheques and postal orders. It is, of course, also the form of buying that puts the buyer at the greatest risk: there cannot be many commonplace acts of faith equal to putting your money in an envelope, dropping it in a box in the street, and then walking away, trusting that after a week or so some goods will appear on your doorstep. It is a tribute to the fundamental honesty of mankind that the system works at all.

Regrettably, the system appeals not only to lawful traders, genuine customers, and publications with advertising space, but also to rogues and simpletons – the former seeing it as a less energetic alternative to bank robbery, and the latter not quite realising just how much business back-up even a simple mail order advertisement needs.

To protect their readers from fraud or failure on the part of the mail order dealers who advertise in their pages, the papers (by which we mean, in this book, both newspapers and periodicals) have set up various schemes designed to ensure that off-the-page mail order customers don't lose their money. These schemes are collectively known as MOPS.

Under the auspices of the Office of Fair Trading, different sections of the press have in the past dozen or so years set up their own MOPS, each run independently of the others, but all broadly intended to serve the same purpose: to refund readers' money if an off-the-page mail order dealer fails to fulfil his obligations for reasons of bankruptcy or liquidation. Some of the schemes also expressly cover claims where the trader has absconded or ceased to trade for some reason other than business failure.

MOPS are in effect insurance schemes, the papers acting as insurers by taking upon themselves the risk of loss that would otherwise be borne by their readers. Like all prudent insurers, they seek to satisfy themselves that the risk they're invited to take is a reasonable one; and if it doesn't seem reasonable, they decline to accept it.

They assess the risk by subjecting the prospective off-the-page mail order advertiser to detailed investigation, requiring him to supply all sorts of information about his business, his product and himself before allowing him to advertise in their pages. Once they have this basic information, they vet it, examine accounts, take up references, seek financial status reports from outside credit agencies, call to inspect stock and premises, and so on. Of course, not all publishers are equally thorough, and not all of them will do all of these things; some of them indeed will do none of them. But no publisher will tell you in advance that his vetting procedures are lax, so prepare yourself for the full treatment.

Even if, after all this, your advertising is deemed acceptable, you may still be required to sign various undertakings guaranteeing to indemnify the publishers if they have to pay out to their readers because of the failure of your business.

The MOPS publishers
The Newspaper Publishers Association (NPA). The NPA is the trade association of the proprietors and publishers of the national daily and Sunday newspapers, together with their associated colour magazines. Although NPA publications are little more than a couple of dozen altogether, they carry about a third of all the off-the-page mail order advertising in the UK.

The NPA's vetting procedures for off-the-page advertisers are probably the most thorough and professional of any of the MOPS, as they are undertaken by a central secretariat instead of being left to individual publishers as is the case with the other MOPS. The scheme is actually operated jointly by the NPA, IPA and ISBA, but it is run on a day-to-day basis by the National Newspapers' Mail Order Protection Scheme Ltd – the secretariat – from whom details and forms may be obtained.

Once a completed application is received from the prospective advertiser, checking procedures take about 28 days, and the application then goes before a management committee which meets weekly. This is the point where the application is either accepted or rejected. Acceptance means that NPA members will be recommended by the committee to accept your advertising, and rejection means that they will be recommended to refuse it. Either way, the final decision rests with the particular paper in which you wish to advertise; it is most unlikely that any paper would override a negative recommendation, as that would leave them financially exposed, but don't assume that a positive recommendation means that you have jumped the final hurdle.

All applications to the MOPS secretariat must be accompanied by a fee ranging from £175 to £5000, depending upon your proposed annual advertising expenditure. These are 1992 rates. The £175 fee is for advertising up to £10,000 a year; the £5000 fee is for advertising in excess of £500,000 a year. The fee is refunded if your application is rejected. If your application is accepted, and your actual advertising expenditure turns out to exceed the value predicted, further top-up fees become payable. Fees paid on the basis of advertising expenditure that falls short of prediction may be either refunded or carried forward to the following year.

Entry into the NPA's scheme is not on a once-for-all basis. You must submit an annual application, and an annual fee, if you wish to continue advertising. The application to renew is less forbidding than the original application, and basically only requires you to indicate any changes that have taken place in the structure or organisation of your business, and to submit a copy of your audited accounts for the year.

The Periodical Publishers Association (PPA). There are about 160 members of the PPA who together publish about 1300 titles, roughly a third of the total number of periodicals published in the UK.

The PPA's MOPS is a rather more commonly agreed policy than a centrally administered scheme. All PAA members use the same application forms to get information from prospective off-the-page advertisers, and they all work to the same guidelines detailing recommended procedures for vetting applicants and upholding MOPS principles. But the actual vetting is left entirely in the hands of the particular publisher approached by the particular advertiser, and this naturally results in a certain unevenness in the application of the policy.

There are no registration fees payable by advertisers, nor any centralised procedure for renewing applications annually.

The Newspaper Society (NS). The NS is the trade association of some 260 proprietors and publishers of regional and local newspapers. Its MOPS policy and practice is similar to that of the PPA.

Except for the purposes of market research, mail order virtually always trawls for customers nationally. While NS papers collectively carry a significant amount of mail order advertising, it is spread rather thinly. The most attractive mail order places for the advertiser are those where there is a concentration of mail order advertising, and the newcomer will probably find himself more concerned with the NPA and the PPA (and non-MOPS publishers – see below) than with the NS.

Scottish Newspapers. The Scottish Daily Newspaper Society and the Scottish Newspaper Publishers Association each has its own MOPS, but members carry very little mail order advertising, and the comments above on the NS apply also to these two Scottish associations.

Non-MOPS publishers
About two-thirds of all periodicals are produced by publishers who are not in any of the MOPS schemes. Their attitude to intending off-the-page advertisers varies from anything as strict as the strictest MOPS publisher right down to 'send us your money and no questions asked'.

Scope of MOPS and non-MOPS schemes

Strictly speaking, the security offered to the mail order purchaser by these protection schemes is very limited. The customer is normally covered only if:

1. He has mailed his payment in direct response to an off-the-page *display* advertisement – that is, an ad paid for by the space occupied rather than by its number of words or lines; and
2. He fails to receive the goods because the dealer has ceased trading.

Different MOPS and different publishers expressly exclude certain advertisements from the protection of the scheme. Although there is no uniformity about the exclusions, they typically relate to classified ads of all kinds, inserts, all forms of two-stage selling, offers of services, products costing 25p or less, garden trees, shrubs, plants, chemicals and fertilisers, goods sold on approval or on COD terms or where the only advance payment required is a small sum to cover carriage costs, certain special seasonal offers, and offers to supply a series of items over time (*collectibles* in the jargon). If your advertising is regarded by the particular publisher as falling under one of these exclusions, you may be spared the full rigours of the MOPS vetting procedures.

Despite the nominally limited protection that MOPS provide, you will see below from the sort of questions put to prospective advertisers and the sort of undertakings demanded of them, that these schemes have a most pervasive influence on the whole mail order operation, setting standards for the maximum delay in order fulfilment, customer refunds, quality of goods, levels of stock, sufficiency of staff, adequacy of premises, availability of service to personal callers, and so on.

Furthermore, while MOPS and other schemes put the media on risk only in the case of display ads selling off the page, publishers increasingly vet *all* display mail order advertisers, and all classified advertisers selling off the page, too. Not surprisingly, the procedures are very similar to the ones already in place for the MOPS and MOPS-type schemes, though they may be applied less rigorously. So unless your mail order methods are restricted to small classified two-stage selling and direct mail, you will probably find yourself having to do battle with forms including at least a selection of questions like those below.

Mail order advertising application forms

Application forms typically ask intending advertisers for three things: information, undertakings, guarantees.

Information

The information required usually includes some or all of the following:

- Applicant's status, ie sole trader, partnership or limited company;
- VAT registration number;
- Name and address under which business is normally carried out;
- Name and address to be given in the proposed advertisement;
- Nature of business premises, eg office, house, shop etc;
- Floor area devoted to the mail order business;
- Number of full-time staff employed;
- Length of time the business has been run from this address;
- Any other names and addresses the business uses or has used;
- Full names and private addresses of all proprietors or directors;
- Amount of capital employed in the business;
- Amount of business capital available;
- Names and addresses of any lenders to the business, plus sums involved;
- Type and extent of insurance cover for both premises and stock;
- If a limited company, registration number and date of incorporation;
- Date of end of accounting year;
- If a subsidiary or associated company, name and address of associated or parent company;
- Address where stock may be inspected;
- Address where main stock is normally kept;
- Nature of premises where main stock is normally kept;
- If goods are to be despatched by another organisation, name and address of that organisation;
- Average stock level;
- Annual sales turnover and pre-tax profit or loss for each of the past, say, three years (together, perhaps, with a copy of the latest audited accounts);
- Name and position of a responsible person at the advertised address who is available to attend to business during normal business hours;
- Name of any person in the business who has ever been associated with any other mail order business or has ever applied to have mail order advertising in any newspaper or periodical; also, the names of the relevant companies, newspapers and periodicals;
- Details of relevant people, companies and circumstances if any

proprietors or directors of the business have been associated with any other business which has ceased trading for any reason;
- Names and addresses of two trade references, ie suppliers from whom business stock has been bought over a period of time;
- Name and address of auditors;
- Name and address of bankers;
- Name and address of solicitors;
- Name and address of advertising agency if employed.

Undertakings

In conjunction with your completed application form you can also expect to be asked to sign an undertaking confirming your agreement to do such things as the following:

- Hold sufficient stock to meet all reasonable demands;
- Supply samples of advertised goods to the advertising media if requested;
- Follow the *BCAP* guidelines;
- Abide by any recommendations of the advertising media;
- Comply with the provisions of all relevant acts, statutes and regulations currently in force;
- Fulfil all orders within a specified period;
- Make full refund to any customer who cancels his order before fulfilment;
- Make full *cash* refund (including p&p) to any customer returning goods within seven days;
- Allow media representatives to inspect the business premises, goods, account books and documents;
- Allow personal callers to inspect and buy goods;
- Notify the media of any changes to the information supplied on the original application form;
- Provide to the media if requested full audited information on the financial position of your business;
- Display the business name prominently at the advertised address.

Guarantees

If despite all the information you give and the undertakings you make, the publisher still feels uncertain about the wisdom of accepting your advertising, and yet is reluctant to refuse it outright, then:

- If yours is a limited company or a partnership, you and the other directors or partners may be asked to sign an undertaking promising, *as individuals*, to indemnify the media in respect of any losses and costs they incur following the failure of your company or partnership to fulfil its obligations.

- You may be asked to provide a bank bond; this is a guarantee by your bank that all losses and costs incurred as above will be paid for.
- You may be required to ensure that all transactions are conducted through a reputable stakeholder who retains customers' money on deposit until you provide him with evidence that the ordered goods have been despatched.
- You may be required to put the whole mail order operation into the hands of a fulfilment house – at your cost, of course.
- You may be invited to offer to supply goods in advance of payment and on approval; in other words, yours would still be a one-stage advertisement but no longer for cash off the page.

Has the beginner any serious chance at all of placing his advertising?

There is no doubt that the media's vetting procedures can be very dispiriting. Without a track record, you will find some of their questions impossible to answer; but if they are left unanswered, the investigator may lack the conventional business indicators – audited accounts, trade references etc – to help him form a rational judgement.

The comment of a spokesman for one of the national papers is worth quoting here. It's a heartening reminder that behind the off-putting forms and procedures, there can be a sympathetic appreciation of the beginner's difficulties. David Soloman of *The Observer* puts the position like this:

> Whilst it is not our wish to stifle new business, we are obliged to protect the reader from the problems which can arise all too frequently in the Mail Order field. Accordingly, I think it only fair to point out that totally new businesses may find it hard to provide a satisfactory application. Ideally we like to see a healthy balance sheet, a good stock position and a reasonable set of references – all of which may be difficult to provide in the early days.
>
> Having said this, each case is treated in its own right. No arbitrary limits are set in respect of stock or asset figures, turnover etc. Nor are we unmindful of the problems posed to new businesses by our fairly stringent requirements. Where possible we will seek further information before turning down an advertisement. A general word of advice to the newcomer would be to accept our investigations with a good grace and to be helpful in the face of requests for further references, stock receipts, product samples etc. Established businesses are required to supply this sort of evidence, too!

So what's to be done?

The first thing is to accept that business is tough. The problems you have in placing your advertising will be repeated in different forms throughout your business career. Help is always most difficult to come by when you most need it, although it may be there in abundance when you don't need it all. A millionaire has no difficulty in getting a sizeable bank overdraft, precisely because he doesn't need one. But if you're scraping along, trying to make ends meet, you could well think from your bank manager's attitude that your modestly overdrawn account is threatening to undermine the whole banking system. It's the same with advertising. Once you're a well established advertiser, you will be constantly pestered by media salesmen wanting to sell you yet more advertising space. But at the start of your business career, *you're* going to have to do the pestering.

Second, prepare your position. Look at the questions you're likely to be asked, and think of ways of dealing with those that you know you can't answer satisfactorily. If, for example, you can't give trade references, set up other referees prepared to testify to your personal integrity and offer these to the media instead, explaining your difficulty.

Third, do understand that the world out there is not monolithic. If your bank manager has refused to lend you money, don't go home muttering to yourself, 'Well, that's that then. Nothing more I can do. The banks won't lend.' That's nonsense. You haven't been dealing with 'the banks'; you have dealt solely with one bank manager. So try another. And another. And another. Every failure is a chance to learn how to refine your approach for the next attempt.

In advertising too, a single rejection is not the end of the world. The press is no more monolithic than the banking system. So try again. But make intelligent decisions about where your next attempt should be.

If the NPA have turned down your off-the-page ad, you ought to know that a further application to an NPA paper is not worthwhile until your business and/or personal circumstances have changed. This is because of the NPA's centralised vetting system; your repeated application will go straight back to the very people who turned down the original one. But if you've been refused by a PPA member or by a paper outside the MOPS altogether, further applications to other papers are decidedly worth making, because each application is dealt with by a different set of people.

Fourth, while it may seem to the newcomer that the media go to great lengths to discourage him from advertising, the truth is that however forbidding their manner, they are really longing to be persuaded that the applicant is a suitable advertiser, because advertising revenue is their life blood. The cover price of a paper goes only part of the way to financing its production: it is advertising money that keeps the show on the road.

Finally, bear in mind that those depressing application forms are ready-printed all-purpose products; they haven't been designed specifically to terrorise *you*. Often enough, a given publisher uses the forms, not because he is particularly seeking answers to all the matters they probe, but merely because he's got a pile of the things on his desk, and sending one off to you is the simplest way he can reply to your initial request to advertise. It is by no means certain that every publisher studies and follows up your replies with the diligence that the original form designer probably had in mind. Sending out a forbidding application form is an easy way of barking menacingly and letting the world know that there's a tough old watchdog in charge. Is one being cynical to suspect that there are some publishers' offices where the returned forms are little more than glanced at, the ferocious beast revealing himself to be an old softie who only wants to be loved? He may need you more than you need him.

Chapter 6

Preparing to Trade

Mail order is one of those businesses where the transition from nothing happening to everything happening can be surprisingly swift and abrupt. If you delay the basic preparations until the need for them becomes urgent, you can cause yourself considerable embarrassment and difficulty. So well before embarking on your first selling campaign, clear the decks for action.

Bring the business into being

Deal with the general business basics discussed in Chapter 4: see that you have adequate business capital, open a business bank account, establish contact with your professional advisers, decide on the legal status of the business, set up a bookkeeping system, decide where you're to operate from, establish sources of trade supply, and prepare to take on staff if appropriate.

Pay particular attention to the following.

Name
Decide what name you're going to trade under. Although a business name has no selling power in mail order – people buy the product not the name – you must have *some* name, and it's worth choosing it with care.

The longer or wordier it is, the more of a nuisance you'll find it for everything from business letterhead design to classified advertising costs. 'The Hop, Skip and Jump People' might seem a distinctive and attractive name for a firm selling outdoor games equipment, but the six-word name would increase the cost of every classified ad you ever run, compared with a one-word name like 'Skippers'. Short names, or ones that may be easily abbreviated, are to be preferred. They're also easier to use on the phone, both when taking and making calls.

Avoid names that are difficult or uncommon or 'clever' or misleading. Since the name has no selling power, the only effect a business name can have is an adverse one if it worries people in some way. So keep it simple and straightforward. If you trade under any other name than your real name, you're legally bound to publish your real name anyway in some at least of your advertising (see page 77), and on your business stationery, so your own real name, either alone or in conjunction with a trade label, eg 'Anne Brown, Fashionwear', is often the best choice.

Address
Make sure that your premises are suitable and adequate for your proposed venture. Even if you run your business from home, you may still need warehouse or storage space elsewhere. However, the address in your advertising and on your stationery will need to be the address at which you actually run your business. Reputable papers refuse to accept advertising that uses an accommodation address, and there are also restrictions on the use of PO Box addresses (see page 77).

Printed business stationery
You need business stationery almost before you need anything else. A small business, especially if run from home, isn't obviously in business at all. If you're to be taken seriously in your first approaches to suppliers, trade associations, agencies and others, you'll find the use of properly printed business stationery a real help.

Most instant print shops on the high street offer a range of standard business stationery layouts, and can do the work quite quickly. Order some printed A4 and A5 letterheads with plain matching envelopes, some compliments slips, and possibly some business cards if you think you'll be calling in person on suppliers and others.

Also useful is a rubber stamp printed with your business name and address. You can use it to put a return address on letters and parcels, to endorse cheques and postal orders to reduce the risk of their going astray when you pay them in at the bank, to mark manufacturers' sales literature as having come from your firm, to stamp on pre-printed order forms and receipts to save the expense of having special ones printed, and so on.

Advertising records
Set up a record-keeping system to monitor the results of your advertising. See pages 156 and 159 for the sort of thing required. These records are distinct from your ordinary business bookkeeping. The latter provides the raw material for assessing the fortunes of the business as a whole. The advertising record enables you to watch and analyse the performance of individual advertising campaigns.

Basic office equipment and materials
Telephone, typewriter and postal scales, plus the usual office accessories – paperclips, folders, paper punch, stapler, ringfiles, cashbooks, duplicate books of order forms and receipts, date stamp etc – are the main

things you'll need to start with. Don't spend money on other equipment or supplies unless you see a real immediate need for them. Franking machines, computerised accounting systems, photocopiers etc may in time be worthwhile but they are an unnecessary drain on the limited resources of a business just starting out in an experimental way. Remember also that virtually every service your mail order business may in due course need can be bought in from an appropriate mailing house.

Product
Decide what you're selling, and satisfy yourself that there will be no problems with continuity of supply.

Set up the basic routines

Whatever the nature of the campaign of the moment, the day-to-day routines of the mail order business remain the same: enquiries and orders are received, replies and goods are sent out. See that these routines are in place before you start trading, or muddle and confusion will rapidly overwhelm you. The routine matters are identified below, together with possible ways of dealing with them in a new, small business. These may or may not suit your own business, but at least take them as a starting point when sitting down to devise systems for yourself.

Orders received
Date-stamp every order and note on it the amount of any payment enclosed, and the key (see page 139) of the press ad or mailshot which has prompted it. For this and for any other notes you write on the order, use a contrasting pen: a red or green felt-tip pen is often suitable as most orders are written in blue or black ballpoint ink. Check that the order details are correct, and if they are not, note the errors prominently on the order.

Before throwing away the outer envelope, make sure it's empty, and that it doesn't include any information missing from the order. Sometimes a customer's name and address are on the back of the envelope but omitted from the order itself; in that case, staple the envelope to the order.

Sometimes a customer writes his name, address and order on the back of his cheque or postal order, with nothing else enclosed. If that happens, copy out the details of the order on a separate sheet and treat this as the customer's order.

Put the order into your 'Orders Received' ringfile, taking care when you punch the holes that you don't punch out any vital information, like the house number.

When all the day's orders are in the file, enter the details in your 'Money Received' cashbook (see page 68): customer's surname, money received, goods ordered (devise a simple coding system for your goods to avoid long narrative entries), and the advertisement key. Total the takings at the end of the day, and transfer details to your Advertising Results Summary (see page 159).

Fulfilling orders

Work through the 'Orders Received' ringfile an order at a time, looking out whatever goods are required, packing them and preparing them for despatch. Once done, mark each order as fulfilled; a prominent tick plus the date will normally suffice.

Under present postal regulations, the cheapest way of mailing packages weighing not more than 750g is the second-class letter post. For packages over 750g but not more than 30kg, the parcel post is best. Over this weight, you will have to use carriers other than the Post Office.

Experiment with packaging to find a quick, cheap and safe method of packing your particular product. The more usual packing materials – corrugated paper, wrapping paper, gummed tape etc – may be obtained from or through local office materials suppliers. It is much cheaper to buy paper products in large rolls designed for commercial use than in the small packets intended for the general public.

Keep selling

Prepare some further advertising material to enclose with all fulfilled orders. Such advertising is almost certainly the cheapest you will ever have. As you are already committed to mailing out the goods, it costs you very little to stuff in some further sales literature – a *free ride* or *piggy back* in the jargon: nothing extra for postage, nothing extra for mailing list rental, nothing extra for envelopes, and the whole thing going to the most up-to-date customer it's possible to imagine. A chance not to be missed.

Receipts

Provided your bookkeeping system allows you to trace an order when the query arises, you can probably dispense with receipts for most non-business customers. If a receipt is needed or requested, a pre-printed receipt form, properly completed and stamped with your business name, will do.

Enquiries

Date-stamp all enquiries and file them in an 'Enquiries Received' ringfile. Although occasionally you will get an enquiry needing its own

91

individually written answer, most enquiries are routine ones, and you should have routine replies available. If your advertising has specifically invited enquiries, then you will, of course, have prepared a specific reply; we look at the contents of such letters in the next chapter. But even unsolicited enquiries can usually be dealt with routinely. Typically the enquirer wants to know what you can supply, for how much, and how he can go about ordering it.

Prepare an all-purpose reply for such enquirers: type a master letter on one of your letterheads, possibly leaving the name-space blank so that you can fill it in later to give the letter at least a suggestion of individuality. The letter should be brief, straightforward, and probably refer to sales literature which you also enclose. Take your letter to an instant-print shop and have a stock of copies made for use as needed.

Work through your 'Enquiries Received' file a letter at a time, marking each as 'done' when you've dealt with it. If you find an enquiry needs an individually written reply, attach a copy of your reply to the enquiry and put both of them into a 'Special Enquiries' file.

Order errors

Some of the orders you receive will inevitably contain errors, but you'll meet the same errors again and again, and so you can set up routines for dealing with them.

The commonest mistakes concern payment. The customer sends the wrong amount of money, or none at all. Or his cheque is wrongly dated or unsigned, or gives one value in words and another in figures, or has been altered but the alterations left unsigned. Sometimes it is not clear precisely what the customer is ordering.

The simplest way of dealing with most order errors is to have a standard letter which acknowledges receipt of the order and then refers the customer to one of the later paragraphs, each of which concerns a different error. A typical example of such a letter is shown opposite. Note that a blank is left for the last paragraph of the letter so that you can write in the appropriate detail if the customer ingeniously commits an error you hadn't thought of in advance.

A seemingly untrappable error occurs when the customer fails to mention his address. Sometimes there is nothing you can do but wait for him to contact you again, probably huffily complaining about your failure to reply. However, if the customer has paid by cheque, you can send one of your standard error letters, addressed to him care of his bank. Put both his name and bank account number on the envelope and mark it 'Please forward' in the top lefthand corner. Paragraph H of the specimen letter is designed to cope with this situation.

MAILERS LTD
23 Somewhere High Road
London N23 32N

Dear

Thank you for your recent order. Please see the
paragraphs I have marked below. I look forward to
receiving your amended instructions in due course.

A   Cheque words and figures differ.

B   Cheque date wrong or unclear.

C   Cheque unsigned.

D   Cheque alterations unsigned.

E   When resubmitting your order, please draw a
    fresh cheque or correct the enclosed cheque and
    sign all alterations.

F   Order underpaid. The balance due is £

G   Our correct prices and terms are shown on the
    enclosed sheet.

H   Please let me know where you want your order
    sent.

I   Your order is unclear. Please re-order.

J

Yours sincerely
MAILERS LTD

Lucy Lockett
Customer Service Dept

Adapt the letter for your own use and have copies made at your local instant-print shop.

Returns

Some of your customers will return the product for refund within a week or two of purchase. Don't quibble. Make a full refund. Send a cheque by return with a compliment slip briefly stating what it's for. Trace the customer's original order: look for his name in your 'Money Received' cashbook to discover the date of his order, and then turn up that order in your 'Orders Received' file. Attach his refund request to the original order, and mark on it the amount you have refunded and the date of refund.

Bouncing cheques

Cheques bounce in two ways. Sometimes your customer's bank will refuse to honour a cheque immediately but suggest that your bank re-presents it; this normally means that the customer's account is not in funds at present but is shortly expected to be so. Although your bank will inform you when this happens, there's no need for you to take any action. Your bank puts the cheque through the system again and if all is well you hear no more about it. At times, however, the dishonoured cheque is returned to you via your bank, and you are left to take the matter up with your customer.

Once again this is a case for a standard letter, though this time one that is freshly typed out on each occasion. Don't let your customer get the impression that he's being dealt with in an impersonal, standardised way, even if he is. Send him his cheque back, say that you've been unable to obtain payment from his bank for it, remind him of the goods you have sent him and when they were sent, and ask him for a fresh payment – in postal orders – by return of post. Be polite but firm.

Usually, that does the trick. But if it doesn't, and the sum involved is relatively small, there's really not much you can do but write it off as a bad debt, and keep a wary eye open for any future orders from that person or that address. If the sum is substantial, follow up with a further and stronger letter in a couple of weeks. And if still nothing happens, consult your solicitor.

Tap into sources of information and help

Post Office

Your local post office will have leaflets detailing the current services and costs of the letter post and the parcel post. For more detailed information on the business services available, contact the appropriate Post Office business in your area: look up in your local telephone directory under Royal Mail (for the letter post), Royal Mail Parcels or Post Office Counters.

It is well worth making early contact with the Royal Mail particularly as they have publications which not only set out their own services but also introduce the beginner to some of the procedures of direct mail.

Mail order associations

Make contact with any of the bodies listed in Chapter 2 who seem appropriate to your business plans. If you get information which you don't need immediately, file it away for future use. It is important to familiarise yourself with the type of information that is readily and often freely available, and to establish contact with associations, and possibly individuals within associations, so that you know where to turn when the need arises.

Specific trade associations

Contact and join a trade association appropriate to the type of products you intend dealing in, ie not a mail order association but one representing the interests of all dealers in your type of goods. Such associations will be able to advise you on the various laws, statutes, codes of conduct etc that concern the particular products, and they will be a continuing source of general business information and advice. Not the least important thing at the start of your business career is that membership of an appropriate trade association helps to establish your business bona fides in the eyes of the world.

If you don't yet know of a suitable association, consult the lists published in various directories, one or other of which will certainly be in a local library. Ask to see *Kelly's Manufacturers and Merchants Directory* or *Whitaker's Almanack* or take the librarian's advice.

Decide how far you can seriously go it alone

Even if you are a creative genius, a talented wordsmith, a gifted designer, and like nothing better than interminably folding enclosures into envelopes, addressing them, sealing them, stamping them and trotting off to the post with them – even then, you will sooner or later need help from one or other of the design, mail and marketing professionals. And if you are a rather more ordinary mortal, you will need that help sooner rather than later.

The distance along the mail order road that you can travel without skilled help is limited. If funds are very tight, you may not be able to afford professional help, and the size and scope of your selling campaigns will necessarily remain modest. Unfortunately, this is one of the conditions in which a very small mail order business is at risk of being permanently trapped. Development is stunted because of lack of professionalism, but professionalism remains expensively out of reach because development is stunted.

What can you do – and what can't you do – for yourself?
The outlook needn't be so gloomy if you recognise your own limitations, and use sensibly such money as you have. Addressing, enclosing, sealing and stamping 10,000 items, for example, is crushingly boring and takes not merely hours and hours but days and days – *and days* – if you try it singlehanded.

Here's an instructive exercise: get 100 envelopes, 100 sheets of paper, and an address book; the phone book will do if you remember that it does not give complete postal addresses. Now start timing yourself. Write or type complete legible addresses on the envelopes, fold each piece of paper twice and pop it into an envelope, seal the envelopes and go through the motions of sticking on 100 stamps. Look at the clock. Now you know how long the very simplest mailing job takes. Multiply the time by 100 to see how long 10,000 would take you. Incredible, isn't it?

But the important point is this: it *can* be done, and the end product is not significantly distinguishable from the work of a professional mailing house. On the other hand, designing the content and preparing the artwork of those 10,000 items is much more exciting and enjoyable, but the difference between the amateur production and the professional one is likely to be glaring, and its consequences depressing for the success of the business. If you can only afford *either* to buy in professional creativity and design *or* professional mail room services, go for the former every time.

Establish contact with service providers
From the DMSSB's *Handbook of Recognised Agencies* (see page 33) you can choose mailing houses which seem to offer the kind of services you need. Get in touch with two or three possibles, discuss your ideas with them, see what ideas they have, and investigate likely costs.

Design studios
It may be that in the early days, the only service you can afford to buy in – and can't afford *not* to buy in – is design. And if this is the only service you're buying, it may be best to buy it locally.

Look up Yellow Pages to find local design studios. If you need artwork prepared either for sales literature or for press advertising, they will be able to help. You can go to them with your own draft ideas, and they will be able to produce sketches – they'll probably call them *visuals* – to give a good impression of what the finished work would look like. They will know about print styles and sizes, and should be able to advise you on all aspects of design. In the end, they will be able to supply you with finished artwork, ready for printing or publishing; and if it is a matter of sales literature, they will be able to advise you about printers, or be able to instruct printers for you.

Your local studio may well be no more expert than you are in the matter of advertising in general or mail order advertising in particular. Don't look to them for advice on these things. They will know nothing about writing sales letters or effective advertising copy. Their speciality is *design*, and they are well worth using if that is what you need. See pages 126–129 for a way of creating advertising on a shoestring, with most of the inspiration from you and most of the technical know-how and artwork from a design studio.

It is almost always better to find a good design studio and take their advice on printing, than to find a good printer and take his advice on design. Printers tend to be better at implementing ideas than initiating them.

An alternative to using an independent design studio
Many of the papers which carry mail order advertising have in-house design facilities which they make available to their advertisers. For your first small venture into display advertising, this is probably the cheapest way of getting professional design help. Some papers do not charge for the service at all; others make only a nominal charge. Of course, there may be an element of take-it-or-leave-it about such design services, and you probably won't be able to sit there with the designer, pushing bits of paper around while ideas take shape. But any professional design help is to be preferred to bumbling along on your own.

Contact the papers

If you are intending to use press advertising of any kind, now is the time to introduce yourself to the advertising departments of those papers which you are likely to wish to use. Don't wait until you are ready to advertise before making a move. As we saw in the last chapter, establishing your business credentials to the satisfaction of the media may in some cases be a lengthy, searching and traumatic experience. Get on with it as soon as possible.

Chapter 7

The Advertising Options

There is a variety of options to be considered before launching an advertising campaign, and indeed even after launching it: Where? When? What? How? all have to be decided. But first and foremost: Why?

Objectives

There is no 'best' form of mail order advertising. The appropriate form is the one that best serves your current objective. This might be to:

- investigate whether there is a market for your product;
- test a particular advertisement;
- build a mailing list;
- make an immediate profit.

Sooner or later, of course, you have to get down to that final objective, but it is by no means always advisable to go for a profit at once. You can't checkmate the king in your opening move at chess, and it is only marginally less difficult to make a killing with your first mail order ad. Unfortunately, the smaller your business, the less chance you have to pursue a careful step-by-step campaign because the cost of experiment and investigation may well exceed your total available capital. If funds are scarce, you may be forced to go for an immediate profit: sink or swim – an exciting business life, though possibly a short one. But if you're more comfortably capitalised, you can pursue a more thoughtful strategy, and your first task in that case is to decide what your current objective really is.

Investigating the market
Suppose, for example, that you have invented a new kind of domestic burglar alarm, with various features not found on any existing products. To have your new device manufactured in quantity would cost a good deal, but the precise unit cost would depend upon how large an order you could give the factory. You have discovered that to get 1000 manufactured would cost you £20 per unit, while an order for 20,000 would bring the unit cost down to less than £10. Question: how many should you order? Answer: probably none at all, without first investigat-

ing what sort of demand there might be for your product, and how much people might be prepared to pay for it.

You could do this by advertising other manufacturers' domestic burglar alarms, and analysing the response in order to get a measure of the demand for such products and the sort of prices people will pay for them. A thousand pounds spent on advertising could buy you a lot of useful information. Even if you lost all of that, it would still be money well spent as it would have saved you an investment of £20,000 or more in a product which you could not have sold. Hopefully, however, the result of your advertising will not be so totally negative, and it will enable you to make sensible decisions about the market, what it requires and what it will pay, and what, therefore, you in your turn can afford to pay for production.

You would be very unlucky indeed not to recover at least part of the cost of such investigatory advertising, but that is incidental to your main current objective – to buy information, *not* to make immediate profits.

Testing an advertisement

Suppose now that you are sure that you have a product that people want, which you can profitably market at a price they are willing to pay. What is the best way to advertise it? If you have done any investigatory advertising, as above, you will already have some pointers, but you still need to test your ideas with the new product to see that you get the best possible return for your advertising money. The objective, as before, is to secure information rather than to make an immediate profit.

Pound for pound of advertising money, how does your success in magazine A compare with magazine B? If you use a Freepost address, does this increase your sales more than enough to cover your increased costs? If you offer to supply goods in advance of payment, does this increase your profits or only your bad debts?

Any number of questions like these may be tested (though only one at a time – see page 151); all you have to do is to run your advertising in two different forms or in two different places and compare the results.

The degree of testing that is practicable depends upon the size of your particular market and the ultimate extent of your intended campaign. If, for example, you are planning to direct mail every household in the country, it makes sense to do test mailings in batches of a few thousand a time, to try out the effects of this piece of advertising literature or that sales letter or whatever, steadily refining your advertising before committing yourself to the big mailing of millions. But with a total mailing list of, say, only 300 names, sample testing would be pointless as the samples would necessarily be so small that the results would be statistically unreliable.

Best is best, but even second-best can be good enough
While you naturally want the best value for money in your advertising, even inferior value may still be worth having if the advertising options are not mutually exclusive. You may find, for example, that magazine A is indeed a more successful medium for you than magazine B, but if B nevertheless shows you a profit, it will still be worth using it, not *instead of* but *as well as* magazine A. The only reason for not running a less profitable ad is if to do so would prevent you from running a more profitable one.

Testing is sensible but not certain
Mail order testing always deals in probabilities rather than certainties. A small-scale test this month before a large-scale campaign next month is unable to test what could well turn out to be the most important variable of all: time. Common sense would tell you that testing an ad for Christmas trees in December will not predict the results of a large-scale campaign in January. But no matter what the product, tomorrow is always different from today, and the influence on your results of such future unknowns as weather, political events, competitive advertising or even the unfathomable workings of chance will never be predictable.

Building a mailing list
All forms of advertising are expensive because the number of potential customers is never more than a fraction of the total number to whom the advertising is addressed. Anything that can be done to target the advertising more precisely must improve results. One way of doing this is to advertise with the specific purpose of building up a list of people likely to be future customers, without worrying about making any immediate profit from them.

Suppose, for example, that you sell expensive limited editions of finely bound books. There are not enormous numbers of people who buy such books, and the cost of advertising a specific title, even in a specialist magazine, may well be prohibitive. A different approach would be not to attempt to sell limited editions direct from magazine advertising, but instead to build up a list of people to whom future direct mailings about such products could be made. Instead of, for example, taking full-page advertising to invite people to send you £250 for your latest collector's item, you could use much cheaper advertising to offer, say, a £5 book *about* collecting fine books and limited editions. By this means you would acquire names and addresses of the very people who are prospects for your expensive products, and in due course you could direct mail them with details of your offers.

It wouldn't matter very much whether the £5 book – the sprat to catch the mackerel – made money or not. If it did, so much the better, but the objective would not be an immediate profit but the building up of a customer list.

Making an immediate profit

This is, of course, the ultimate objective of the whole business but not, as we have seen, necessarily the current objective of any particular piece of advertising. Even when it *is* the current objective, you still have to choose between one-stage and two-stage selling.

One-stage selling

One-stage selling aims to make an immediate sale, with no further information being supplied to the customer before he commits himself to a purchase. Selling off the page in the press is an example of it, but there is an exactly comparable form of selling in direct mail, leaflet distribution, and indeed in all other possible forms of advertising that mail order can use, hence the more all-embracing term *'one-stage selling'*. Its essence is that the entire sales message – product, price, ordering procedure – is delivered in one package, whether in the press, by post, on TV, or however.

If you use one-stage selling, you can expect to have customers' money to pay into the bank within the week. And before a fortnight is up, you'll know whether your advertising is working satisfactorily or not.

Two-stage selling

In two-stage selling, you invite the public to send to you for further details of your product, and your intention is to make sales by means of the message you send in reply.

Two-stage selling is always a more long-winded business than one-stage selling, and success or failure takes longer to make itself plain. The two advantages of two-stage selling relate to the lesser cost of the first stage of the process, compared to one-stage selling, and the greater flexibility a reply mailing provides for you to develop your sales message as fully as you wish.

The cost advantage is most marked if the first stage is in the press. Even a relatively cheap classified ad can pull enquiries for a relatively expensive product, whereas an attempt to sell off the page might require a large and expensive display advertisement.

The advertised offer

The advertised offer is the total 'package' you enticingly display before your potential customers. The main part of the package is, of course, the product itself, but what determines whether the product sells or not is the way it's packaged: its price, terms of payment, ways of ordering, and so on. In all of these, too, you have options.

Price

Next to the product itself, price is obviously the most crucial part of your advertised offer. Various aspects of pricing have already been dealt with in Chapter 3, and these should be borne in mind when reading the following comments.

Take as your starting point the unit cost to you of the product and multiply it by three. Does this price seem discouragingly high? If it does, reconsider your product choice. If it doesn't, well and good. If, by contrast, it seems, from the prospect's point of view, ridiculously cheap, then choose a higher price which is merely attractively cheap.

To give your price the final sparkle before putting it on display, polish off a penny or two if by doing so you can shift it to the favourable side of one of the psychological price dividers that occur at the round figures. A product priced at £9-something, for example, seems substantially cheaper than one priced at £10-something, even if the exact figures are £9.99 and £10.01. Somehow, the difference between two such prices seems much greater than the difference between, for example, £8.67 and £8.69. The reason is that people tend to think of the pounds rather than the pence when considering a possible purchase. Indeed, you may well decide that if you can't mark your product down to the next lower price ending in 99p then you might just as well mark it up to the next higher price ending in 99p.

Whatever decision you make, it will only be provisional, and may need to be modified to take account of some of the other features considered below, and in the light of your experience once you start to run your advertising.

Post and packing (p&p)

The question is this: should you incorporate the p&p cost within the product price or should you identify it separately? Should you, for example, offer your product for *£4.50 (plus 70p p&p)* or simply for *£5.20?* The latter is neater, uses fewer words (an important consideration in classified advertising at least) and is less likely to lead to error among customers of uncertain arithmetical skill. The former, on the other hand, has the advantage of making the product seem cheaper, because few people take p&p into account while at the stage of wondering whether a product is worth buying or not.

On balance, it is usually better to identify the p&p charge separately. In display advertising and illustrated sales literature you can have the best of both worlds by featuring the product price prominently in the main part of your sales message, with the p&p charge appropriately and less discouragingly included in the ordering instructions.

Payment terms
The easier and less risky you can make it for your customers to pay, the more sales you can expect. Unfortunately, anything that makes your payment terms more attractive to your customers also makes them less attractive to you. So choose with care.

Cash with order (CWO)
The simplest and, from your point of view, the best payment terms. The customer sends a cheque or postal orders at the time he places his order, so you have his money in your hands before parting with the goods. Postal orders are normally totally secure. If you have any doubts about cheques, allow 10 days after paying them into your bank before despatching the goods; a bad cheque will have bounced by then (see page 94).

Cash on delivery (COD)
This is safer for your customer, more troublesome for you, and more costly for both of you. The customer places his order either by letter or phone, and pays the postman or other carrier when the goods are delivered; the carrier than remits the payment to you. If you send your goods by post, you have to complete a special form for each package and hand both form and package across a post office counter. If you use the parcel post, you have the normal postage plus the COD fee of £1.60. If you want to use the letter post, the package will only be accepted as a first-class registered item, which means a registration fee of £1.90 in addition to the first-class postage and the COD fee (1992 rates).

Suppose your packed goods weigh a bit over 700g – the weight of two or three typical paperbacks – and your packaging costs you 10p, then your p&p costs are about £1.50 in the ordinary second-class post, £4.20 in the COD parcel post, and £5.45 in the COD letter post. If your product price is, say, £10, then these p&p costs are respectively 15, 42 and $54\frac{1}{2}$ per cent on top of that product price. These last two are hefty additions, and they suggest that COD is only worth considering if your product price is high enough to make the extra fees seems reasonable – say, £25 or more. Contract customers of the Post Office benefit from a slightly lower COD fee – £1.20 at 1992 rates – but the conclusion remains the same: COD is a realistic option only for higher priced items.

Non-Post Office carriers may also offer you COD facilities, but the relative cost considerations are likely to be similar to those above.

Giving credit

There is little doubt that offering to send goods in advance of payment will boost the number of orders you receive. But there are three tricky problems that credit selling gives rise to: (a) deciding upon the creditworthiness of those who place credit orders; (b) ensuring that you receive the payments due to you; and (c) financing your business while waiting for payments to come in. All three problems can be solved, but only at the cost of extra business organisation and extra money. Wait till your business is well established before trying to weigh up the advantage of supplying on credit against the disadvantage of having to underwrite the risk.

On approval. In effect all mail order goods are sent on approval. *BCAP*, for example, stipulates that purchasers should be able to return goods for refund within seven days of receipt. However, expressly advertising to supply goods on approval is generally understood to mean that you will supply them in advance of payment: as already indicated, that is probably not a good system for you in the early days.

Accepting credit cards

Credit cards are attractive alike to buyer and seller. They permit a customer to order by letter or phone, the credit card company guaranteeing the seller that payment will be made, while at the same time affording the buyer some degree of security against the seller's possible default. Additionally, of course, the buyer enjoys the opportunity of making purchases beyond his immediate cash resources, and if he does so, the seller finds that rather enjoyable too.

Barclaycard and Access alone have something like 14 million cardholders between them, a very sizeable section of any seller's market.

But, of course, there are difficulties for the new mail trader. Before accepting you into their schemes, the credit card companies normally look for a business track record of at least a year. They will probably not be too happy if individual transactions are typically less than £10, or if your total expected volume of credit card business is below about £4000 a year. If they do accept you, you will have to pay a joining fee of about £50 and a commission of anything up to 4.5 per cent of your credit card sales.

Treat all the above figures as rough guidelines only; in all cases it comes down to a matter of negotiation between you and the companies. But as to whether the schemes are worth joining if you can, the unqualified answer must be: yes. Enquire at the business desk of any high street bank for information about their card schemes.

Part payments
This is a compromise between CWO and credit, and the comments made above about those two payment terms apply here also. The customer sends only part of the purchase price with his order, undertaking to pay the balance within a certain period after receiving the goods. This makes the transaction seem less risky to the customer, and so encourages him to send for something he might be hesitant to order on full CWO terms. By the same token, of course, it is more risky for you. If you offer such terms, you should ensure that the initial payment at least equals your cost price and delivery expenses so that if the customer defaults on later payments, you will not be financially worse off than if he had not ordered at all.

Other inducements to buy

Anything that reduces the customer's cost or risk or difficulty in ordering, or increases the value or rarity of what he gets for his money, is likely to improve the number of orders received. The main inducements are represented by the price of the product itself and the terms of payment. But other minor inducements may just tip the balance your way. Not all of them can be used in all forms of advertising. Your common sense will tell you what is and isn't possible – you obviously can't include an order form in a classified advertisement, for example.

Money-back guarantee
This is one of the phrases that mail order has given to the English language – and one it can well be proud of. It is quite extraordinary to what lengths high street shops will sometimes go to avoid refunding to dissatisfied customers. Here at least mail order shows the way. It may be a commonplace of mail order advertising: *BCAP* and the MOPS may require it whether it's stated or not; the general public may expect it as a matter of course. But still, *always* mention the money-back guarantee. You're going to make refunds to dissatisfied customers anyway, so why not say so? The words are comforting to prospective customers, and their use is one of the simplest ways of attempting to turn ditherers into purchasers.

Free offers
Offering the purchaser something additional to the main product at no extra cost can be a powerful inducement to buy. *BCSPP* warns about the possible misuse of the word 'gift', and both it and the *BCAP* require that anything described as 'free' should be genuinely so, and that the price of a related product should not be increased in order for the 'free' offer to be made.

However, we all know that nothing in life is free – *somebody* has to pay for it; and in all businesses except those that go bust, that 'somebody' is the customer. If you build the free gift into your advertised offer from the start, you will be able to pitch your product price accordingly without giving offence to anyone. If you add the free gift at a later stage, as a refinement to your offer, you should hold your product price steady, and aim to recoup the increased costs – and indeed enhance your profits – from the additional sales generated by the inducement.

While all markets are different, free offers work best if they have a genuine appeal to the purchaser of the main product. A piece of jewellery offered to purchasers of handbags, or blank cassettes with cassette recorders are the sort of offers to consider. Some advertisers seem to succeed with seductive offers of 'mystery' free gifts; and although the mystery, once revealed, is frequently trivial and disappointing – a packet of needles or a plastic comb are typical – the promise still retains its allure for some purchasers. Study the other advertisers in your own market and see what they're up to.

Limited offers

Most mail order purchases are made on impulse. Your customers buy your product not because they have reflected long and hard on the matter, and have got up that morning thinking, 'Right, today's the day I'm going to send off for one of those Whatsits'; it doesn't work like that at all. Your advertising forces itself upon the prospect's attention, either because it happens to be on the page of the paper he's looking at, or because it's something that's just dropped through the door. If your sales message interests him at all, his most likely response is to think that he might do something about it later; but 'later' almost never comes. Other things catch his attention, and your advertised offer is forgotten. If it is to succeed, it must succeed *now*.

One way of inducing immediate action is to put a limit upon your offer. This could, for example, be a time limit: *We're giving away six – yes, six! – cassettes absolutely free with all orders received by 28 February.* Or a stock limit: *We have only a limited number of Whatsits at this ridiculous price, and orders will be dealt with on a strictly first-come-first-served basis.*

Whatever the limit, it must be a genuine one; and that makes it something of a two-edged sword. While it may effectively create a sense of urgency, and thus produce a number of sales that might otherwise have been lost, it may also prematurely kill off the ad so that anyone noticing it for the first time after the deadline may well be discouraged from ordering anything at all.

Order form
The inclusion of an order form in your advertised offer, like the reply envelope considered below, is less an inducement than its absence is a disincentive. Without it, the customer must find some paper to write on, work out how to say what he wants, and make sure he writes it down clearly and unambiguously. For most people, these are not among the most challenging tasks in the world, but for some they are. And for everyone, an order form that may need no more than the writing in of one's name and address definitely simplifies the ordering procedure. All the customer needs is a pen. He may be able to complete the form immediately he has read the ad. No need to go in search of other materials, risking being sidetracked by a demanding cat, a chatty child or by any of the other siren voices that seduce prospective customers from the straight and narrow path that leads to your order book.

Envelope
You can provide an envelope for your customer in a number of ways, and all of them offer at least a marginal advantage in cost and convenience to him. Equally, they all add to your own costs, and, as with so much else in mail order, the balance of advantage in any particular case is only to be ascertained by testing.

Printed unstamped envelope. This is the simplest and cheapest offering you can make. The customer will still have to find a stamp, but he is saved the chore of finding an envelope and writing out the address.

Printed stamped envelope. This is the next simplest but by far the most expensive of the offerings you can make. By putting a postage stamp on the reply envelope you enclose with your advertising, you exert a slight moral pressure on the customer, possibly making him feel that it is 'only fair' to send you a reply since you have gone to the trouble of sending him a stamp for the purpose. But if that moral pressure is resisted, you have done nothing but push up your advertising costs by 18p a prospect. It may still be worth your while if you're selling an expensive product with a substantial profit margin, but probably not otherwise.

Royal Mail Response Services. The Royal Mail Response Services Licence entitles you to use the Business Reply Service and the Freepost Service. The difference between the services is described below, but both enable your customers to write to you without having to pay the postage themselves. The licence costs £55 a year, and the licensee is charged the standard postage plus $\frac{1}{2}$p for each item delivered. You have to keep your account with Royal Mail in credit by making regular payments in advance of the expected charges you will incur. At the time of setting up the licence, a minimum advanced payment of £37 is required in addition to the £55 annual fee. (All fees quoted are 1992 rates.)

The Business Reply envelope has to be pre-printed – by your own printers – to design specifications laid down by Royal Mail. You can opt for either first-class or second-class post, but whichever you choose, your Business Reply letters will normally come in the second rather than the first postal delivery of the day. If you wish, however, you can opt for the Priority Response Service at a cost of a further $\frac{1}{2}$p per item delivered, and your letters will then normally come in the first delivery of the day. Whether you use the Priority Service or not your outlay will be significantly less than pre-stamping reply envelopes as you have to pay postage only on items actually delivered to you.

The Freepost service is available only in the second-class post but otherwise works in a more flexible way than the Business Reply service. While you can, if you wish, provide your customers with your own printed envelopes – as with the Business Reply service – you can also quote your Freepost address in your advertising so that the customer can use it when writing to you on his own stationery. This means, for example, that you can use a Freepost address in your classified advertising.

There is a slight risk in a Freepost address in that it is available for anybody who wishes to write to you on any matter, even if they are doing so just as a joke or to make a nuisance of themselves, and you have an open-ended commitment to pay for all replies. With the Business Reply service, on the other hand, the only people who can use your stationery are those to whom you have deliberately chosen to supply it.

Customer's stamped addressed envelope. In two-stage advertising, you may wish to consider asking the customer to supply *you* with a stamped and self-addressed envelope (SAE) for your reply. Such a request would hardly be an inducement for people to write in for further details – indeed it would be a positive discouragement for them to do so. But there are times when a negative inducement of this kind does serve your purpose.

As always, it comes down to arithmetic. The cost to you of sending replies to enquirers will sometimes be a significant part of your total advertising bill. It may be that if the customer pays the reply postage, an unprofitable advertising campaign can be turned into a profitable one. This is more likely to be the case if your product is very low-priced, and you find that the number of enquirers who go on to make a purchase is rather low. It could be that the first stage of your two-stage advertising is attracting too many frivolous enquirers, people not seriously in the market for your product who send off for details out of idle curiosity and because it costs them so little to do so. Requiring them to send an SAE for details may be just enough to put them off, and so improve the overall quality of your enquirers and therefore the percentage who go on to make a purchase. Thus, asking for an SAE may in some cases help you to target your advertising more effectively.

The media

Though there are many advertising media, just two of them overwhelmingly account for most mail order business done in this country: the press and the post. These two are considered in some detail in following chapters. Here we briefly run through all the options open to you, with their pros and cons.

The press

Press advertising allows you to put your sales message before a large number of people very quickly and very easily – at least once you've cleared the MOPS hurdles.

Advertising in the main dailies, Sundays and periodicals reaches the *national* market, and there is very little point in being in mail order and bothering with anything less than the national market. Advertising in local newspapers, however relatively cheap it may look, is just not worth it. But you don't need to learn any rules about where it's worth advertising and where it isn't, or to try to work things out for yourself from first principles. Just look at where other regular mail order dealers are advertising – that's where you want to be.

One of the disadvantages of press advertising is that its cost is broadly related to the circulation figures of the paper concerned, and not to the number of readers likely to be interested in what you have to sell. A large part – and in the case of the non-specialist papers like the national dailies and weeklies, a very large part – of your expenditure is just money down the drain.

Suppose, for example, that you're selling a product of interest to hamster owners. There must be a good number of those, and all of them can be thought of as prospects. But an even greater number of people *don't* own hamsters and therefore cannot be in the market for your product at all. in fact, something like one person in 12 owns a hamster; that means that your ad in a popular national newspaper with a readership of 6 million would interest a potential maximum of only 500,000 people; the other 5,500,000 people would be of no value to you at all. Or put it another way: if your advertisement costs you £400, you know from the start that eleven-twelfths of that – about £367 – is just thrown away because you are spending it to get your sales message to people who are not remotely interested in what you are selling.

Even if you place your advertisement in a specialist magazine, aimed specifically at hamster owners, so that you could fairly assume that 100 per cent of the readership owned or were about to own a hamster, you will still waste a proportion of your money because large numbers of people never buy *anything* by mail order.

None of these observations, of course, means that press advertising is inadvisable; indeed, along with direct mail, it's the mainstay of mail order. But don't overlook its weaknesses; seek to minimise them by giving careful thought to the appropriateness of the places you advertise to the products you are selling.

Editorial reviews

A number of newspapers and journals and, indeed, radio and TV programmes, regularly run features which draw the public's attention to new and interesting products. Though the effect may be the same as that of an advertisement, such editorial comment differs from advertising in that you neither pay for it nor have any control over what is said. It is not worth spending a lot of time and energy trying to get favourable write-ups or reviews. If you get one, regard it as a bonus; they can never be the cornerstone of your advertising policy. However, if you know of a regularly appearing feature that seems appropriate to your product, you have little to lose by sending the editor details of what you are selling and why you think it may be of special interest to the public he serves. Don't forget to enclose full ordering details; a favourable review that quotes the wrong price or fails to mention the p&p charge can cause you more trouble than it is worth.

Beware of being persuaded to buy advertising space in a paper on the understanding that your product will also get an editorial mention. If the paper is a good place for you to advertise, you will want to advertise there anyway; if it's not a good place, the editorial write-up won't improve it.

Direct mail

The major strength of direct mail is that your advertising goes only to specified individuals. Provided that the list of individuals you use has been carefully compiled and maintained, none of your money is wasted – as it invariably is in press advertising – sending your sales message to people who are definitely never going to buy your product.

Consider again the hamster example. If you could get a list of hamster owners who have in the recent past actually bought pet products by mail, you could post your advertising literature direct to exactly the sort of people you want to reach.

A further advantage is that you can get much more information into a mailshot than into a press advertisement. The cost of press advertising is roughly proportionate to the size of the advertising space; if a given ad costs £50, another 10 times the size is likely to cost £500. Direct mail costs, however, do not increase in the same simple fashion. Apart from printing – whose unit costs, anyway, decline as volume increases – it costs no more, for example, to mail an A4 sheet crammed both sides with information than to mail the same sheet with just a single sentence on it.

There are, of course, disadvantages too, but more of this in Chapter 10.

Door-to-door leaflets

Door-to-door leaflet distribution is cheap but indiscriminate, your sales message going to all the households of a particular area with no account being taken of the different interests and inclinations of the people in those households. This form of advertising is probably appropriate only for products likely to interest householders *as* householders – house security devices, decorating aids etc. There are, however, systems of area classification which aim to identify where there are concentrations of people likely to be responsive to particular promotions. These are known as geodemographic systems and you may like to consider them if household leafleting appeals to you. See also page 147.

However, as has been said already, mail order is a nationwide business, and both press advertising and direct mail can put you in touch with the national market. While it is possible to conduct door-to-door advertising on a national scale, to do so would involve millions of households, and despite the relatively low unit costs, the scale and expense of such an operation rules it out for most mail order ventures. Even if your costs are not more than £20 per 1000, a campaign to reach 5 million households would set you back £100,000, and you would still not have reached the national market of upwards of 30 million households.

If, despite this, you think that the method might be particularly suitable for your product, you can conduct a very cheap experiment by pushing your leaflets through 1000 letterboxes in the nearest town. And if you want to scale up the operation, contact agencies that specialise in household distribution – look up the *DMSSB Handbook*. The Post Office also has a Household Delivery Service in which unaddressed items are delivered along with the ordinary mail.

Radio and TV

Although these have been used for mail order advertising, the beginner would do well to keep clear of them. You can get through your advertising money at alarming speed, and you depend upon your potential customers having pen and paper handy to jot down – and jot down correctly – price, address, phone number and other ordering information before your message vanishes into the ether.

Prestel and other interactive electronic media
These have not yet established themselves in a big enough way to make them suitable for mail order to the general public. They are perhaps worth considering only if your product appeals specifically to those enthusiasts who are already hooked up to electronic mailboxes and other marvels of the moment.

Chapter 8
Creating an Advertisement

The fact that UK advertisers, in and out of mail order, spend about £4000 million of their advertising money every year through the advertising agencies is proof enough that the agencies have a professionalism and expertise that is worth the buying. As pointed out in Chapter 6, the extent to which you can hope to create and run your own advertising campaigns without professional help is limited. And the limits are nowhere more obvious than in the business of creating the advertisement itself, whether a display ad in the press, a page in a catalogue for direct mailing, a sales letter or whatever.

This chapter can't turn you into an expert in copywriting, typography or design. But then as a mail order dealer, it's no more your job to produce your own advertising than it is to manufacture your own product or draw up your own contracts of employment. You may do these things, of course, if you choose to and you have the appropriate knowledge and skills. But your real function as a dealer is to be the conductor of the orchestra, not one of the first violins.

That being said, it could be that in the early stages of your business, shortage of cash may oblige you not only to answer your own phone, lick your own stamps and make your own tea, but also to create your own advertising – at least to the extent of dreaming up the ideas, even if you put the execution into professional hands. And this, indeed, is probably your best way of compromising between a lack of funds and a lack of skill.

Whether your advertising is DIY or professional, it *is* part of your function as a dealer to understand the principles upon which good practice is based; the conductor may be a lousy violinist himself, but he needs to know what a good violinist can do, and to recognise it when he's done it.

There are obvious differences between, say, a four-line classified ad inviting enquiries and a full-page colour supplement ad selling off the page. Less obvious is that any two such ads have a great deal in common, not only with each other but also with all other mail order advertising. They share certain principles of construction and expression.

Structure

All mail order advertising, from small ads to full-page displays to direct mail letters, have the following common structural elements:

- *the headline* which first attracts attention;
- *the sales message* which makes clear what is being offered and what its merits are; and
- *the call to action* which tells the reader what he must do to accept the offer.

The headline

Some dedicated would-be buyers scan column after column of advertising, reading every single word. Most people, however, just cast an eye down the page and only stop to read in detail when something catches their attention. That 'something' is the headline, hence its importance. If you can't grab your reader with the headline, then you've lost him for ever; the rest of your ad may be brilliant and compelling, but he'll never know if the headline didn't stop him in the first place.

The headline is the bait that attracts the fish, and you make it up on the basis of the particular fish you hope to catch. An important point to grasp, though at first a surprising one, is that you are *not* concerned to attract the attention of a majority of readers: your aim is to attract the attention of those readers who are likely to be in the market for the product. Be specific. Think who your likely customers are and write a headline for *them*.

Match the headline to the customer

Here is an example of an inappropriately eye-catching headline: *CUT-PRICE WHISKEY ruins your health. Make your own fruit juice instead with our latest high-speed juice extractor.* You can see what's wrong. The people attracted by the *CUT-PRICE WHISKEY* headline are probably not in the market for the product, and the people in the market for the product are probably not attracted by the headline. It's no good attracting, say, 80 per cent of the readership with your headline if your likely customers are all to be found among the remaining 20 per cent.

A better headline for the juicer might be: *MAKE 100% FRUIT JUICE AT HOME – pure, healthy, fast, cheap – with the latest Jucermatic.*

Remember: headlines must be designed to attract the maximum number of likely customers, not the maximum number of people in general.

Be simple and serious

If you're writing your own copy, avoid 'clever' headlines, puns, jokes and other witticisms. (*Copy*, by the way, is advertising jargon for the words and/or pictures that make up an advertisement.) Even the professionals can make mistakes here; it's a dangerous area. There is always the risk that something you find brilliantly funny will strike the reader as weak, hackneyed or even offensive; worse, he may fail to see the joke at all and totally misunderstand what you're saying.

Target your headline

Avoid generalities which, designed to appeal to everybody, in fact get through to nobody. Frantic headlines like *FABULOUS OFFER!* or *AMAZING BARGAIN!!!* do nothing to sort out potential customers from the rest; and past advertisers have so overworked such claims that they attract as little useful attention as burglar alarms ringing outside shops. We're all so used to them sounding off without cause that we no longer take any notice.

Target your headline to speak directly to each individual prospect. Questions which invite the answer 'yes' often make good headlines: *LOOKING FOR A NEW CAMERA?*, *GARDEN OVERGROWN AGAIN?*, *CAN YOU TYPE?*, *BORED WITH YOUR JOB?* and so on. 'Commands' can also be effective: *CUT YOUR MORTGAGE REPAY-MENTS BY HALF*, *STOP WASTING MONEY ON SHOE REPAIRS*, *RUN YOUR OWN BUSINESS*, *ENJOY YOUR RETIREMENT* etc. In both questions and commands, the word *you* and its derivatives are either expressed or very strongly implied, and it is this that makes the reader feel personally addressed.

The principle of personal address

Making your potential customer feel that you're talking directly to him is of the greatest importance in all forms of advertising. While you as the seller are optimistically thinking of the thousands of people out there, each of those people is thinking only of himself. Your words impinge upon him most effectively if he feels you're talking directly to him as an individual. You remember how the unamused Queen Victoria complained that her prime minister spoke to her as if she were a public meeting. Everyone dislikes being harangued, and if your advertising gives that impression, it will tend to be ignored.

Take an example from a non-mail order form of advertising. Imagine a street trader selling balloons. He stands in the same place for hours, and possibly thousands of people pass by him. If he were to shout, 'Balloons for sale! Balloons here for everybody!', a certain number of passers-by hearing the cry would think. 'That's a good idea – I'll get one for little Whatsit.' But many other people, who could be potential balloon-buyers, would hear the trader's cry but not relate it to themselves in any way, and they would pass on without considering the matter at all. Suppose, however, the trader were to try a different technique. What if he identified likely balloon-buyers from among the people walking past his pitch, say, anyone accompanied by a small child? When such a person came within speaking distance, the trader could say directly to him, 'Balloon for the kiddie? Only 20p.' The passer-by, feeling himself personally addressed, would have to make a definite decision – to buy or not to buy. He couldn't just shut his mind to the whole thing as when the trader was crying his wares to the world at large.

While press and postal advertising lack the personal presence of the street trader, they are still governed by the same principles of human behaviour, and you will sell more successfully if each of your prospects feels as if you were talking directly to him.

Match the headline to the page
Keep in mind the particular context in which your advertising is to appear, and consider whether the reader is likely to be positively seeking a particular purchase or just idly glancing down the page. If you were trying to get enquiries from possible buyers of bicycles, for example, your ad in the Personal column might begin *STOP PAYING FARES*. Travel free. . . . But the same headline under a Bicycles for Sale classification would be inappropriate because people looking at such a column are plainly already sold on the idea of buying a bicycle, and it is only the product itself, its price and other inducements which will dispose them to read one ad rather than another.

What it comes to is this: if your prospect is positively looking for the type of thing you are selling, it may be enough for your headline merely to announce that you are selling it. If, on the other hand, you believe that you must persuade the reader that he has a need which your product can satisfy, then your headline should relate to the need rather than the product.

Headlines in illustrated advertising
In display advertising, direct mail leaflets or ad pages in a catalogue, a headline may be purely verbal, as in the above examples, partly verbal and partly pictorial, or even – though this is the least likely – entirely pictorial. What makes the headline a headline is that it is the part of the advertisement designed to catch the reader's eye.

Headlines in direct mail
A mailshot is normally composed of a number of items. While some of the items are advertisements in their own right, showing the usual three-part structure, they also collectively form a single advertisement: the

116

mailshot. And a mailshot in its totality exhibits the same three-part structure, with the letter usually functioning as, in effect, the headline of the entire package.

The sales message

The sales message, encouraging the acceptance of your offer, need not be grammatically separate from the headline or the call to action. A combined headline and sales message is often seen in brief classified ads. Here's an example from the DIY column of a weekly magazine: *PRECISION MITRE CLAMP, only £2.25 from . . .* and from the Printing Services column *RUBBER STAMPS, fast service, free catalogue. . . .* In both cases the headline is simply the first part of the sales message, the advertisers assuming that it is enough merely to name their products in view of the specialist nature of the columns in which they are advertising.

The function of the sales message is to say what the product is and what it does in such a way that people will want to buy it or send for further details of it. The headlines having caught the reader's attention, the sales message must quickly tell him something that ties in with it or he will glance away at something else. The sales message must satisfy the curiosity aroused by the headline.

Facts and benefits

The sales message concerns itself with two things: what the product *is* and what it can *do* for the customer – the facts and the benefits. It's generally best to lay more stress on the benefits, referring to the factual specification of the product to support your claims.

Consider this example: *SPARKLING WHITE TEETH are yours when you use X's new toothpaste with the jeweller's polish ingredient. Sample tube from. . . .* What the advertiser is offering here is not really the toothpaste but the implied sparkling smile: what the product *is* is subordinated to what it *does*. People are prompted to buy, not so much for the product itself but for what it will do for them or make them into.

This is an important principle. Just as people buy aspirin from a chemist to relieve a headache, not because they are passionately fond of aspirin or concerned about its composition, so they will buy all sorts of other products for the benefits they believe they will thereby gain. They have it at the back of their minds that their pain, discomfort or unhappiness will be reduced, or their pleasure, well-being or happiness enhanced. If someone believes that by making a simple purchase he will bring about a favourable alteration, however small, in his life, he will be strongly disposed to make such a purchase. It is the task of the sales message to convince the prospect that the product can indeed do just that.

117

Convincing the customer

To convince someone that a product can confer a valuable benefit upon him, you must take account of the things he values in life. While different people value different things, there is perhaps a common factor that lies behind the diversity: a wish to be the sort of person that others admire.

People want to be rich, powerful, beautiful, accomplished, clever, strong, skilful, charming, and so on, and they want the possessions that give them these qualities or that help to announce to the world that they have them. Above all, they want money. While most people profess the view that money isn't everything, they also secretly believe that, in their own case at least, it will buy most of the things that it isn't.

So advertising frequently stresses the money that can be saved or made by a particular purchase. And it often more subtly implies that you will be one of the envied few if you drink a certain beer, drive a certain car, use a certain hairspray, buy a certain book, and so on. The psychology of sales messages is the same whether you are selling vermouth on television or brass buttons in *Exchange & Mart*.

Pictorial sales messages

As with headlines, the sales message of a display ad, leaflet, catalogue page etc may be expressed, in part at least, in the illustration. This is most obviously the case when the look of the product is a major selling feature – fashionable clothes, jewellery, ornaments, decorations, and so on.

The call to action

Every mail order advertisement must tell the customer what he has to do if he wants to accept the offer. Your instructions should be clear, explicit and simple. It's unforgivable to lose your customer at this stage through thoughtlessness. To have got him this far and then have him slip away on a technicality, perhaps because he doesn't know who to make his cheque payable to or whether you accept postal orders (and people *do* worry about these things), is like having a full card and not calling bingo. Is your address clearly shown? If money is to be sent, does the customer know precisely how much? Have you said if the p&p charge is per item or per order? If your advertising includes a coupon for the customer to complete, has he got enough room to write in the information you're asking him for? And is it absolutely clear *what* information you're asking for?

And remember this too: many people will read a particular ad, think to themselves that it really sounds interesting and that they'll do something about it shortly, and then put the matter out of their minds for ever. The call to action is really a call to action *right now*. Look back at pages 105–109 for some of the inducements you might use to minimise the risk of losing your customer at this stage.

Expression

Language
The principle of personal address has already been referred to. You make each of your readers feel that you are talking directly to him by the use of the word *you* and its derivatives, expressed or implied, and by the general immediacy of your language. Use everyday words, and prefer the concrete to the abstract, the dynamic to the static, the active to the passive.

Don't write *A WHOLE ROOM MAY BE DECORATED with a substantial time saving over conventional methods by the employment of X's Auto-Paint Machine. A cost saving in excess of 50% may also be effected.* Prefer instead *PAINT A WHOLE ROOM IN UNDER TWO HOURS with X's new Auto-Paint Machine – and cut your costs in half at the same time.*

Try to use action verbs – *save* money, *cut* costs, *paint* your house, *speak* fluent French etc.

There are some words that seem to have a special magic in advertising, words like *new*, *free*, *save* and related and similar words, and you should use them freely whenever appropriate.

On the other hand, there are words which are definitely to be avoided. Any word that your prospect cannot understand is likely to make him stop reading your advertisement then and there. So use everyday language. You cannot persuade unless you are first understood.

Letters
In mail order, the principle of personal address is nowhere manifested more plainly than in letter-writing. The letter is the most natural form of direct address to use in the mailing context. Everyone is familiar with it as a purely personal document, and even when the recipient can plainly see that it has not been written specially for him, he still tends to bring to it something of the personal attention he would normally give to his private correspondence.

Thanks to computer technology, it is now easy to match in the recipient's name and address with the printed letter although, for the illusion to be complete, the letter itself should be printed in a matching typewriter-like typeface. Matching in is the most powerful way of individualising a letter. You can hardly give a stronger impression of speaking directly to someone than by addressing him by name.

Even though it is now possible to produce duplicated letters that look like individually written ones, there has developed a style of direct mail letter composition which makes such letters utterly unlike anything found in the real world of normal correspondence. Some of the major direct mail advertisers consistently produce letters in the form of four-page folders, printed in two or more colours, repeating the prospect's name in the main text of the letter and using all sorts of display devices to drive the sales message home. None of these things is ever found in a genuine, individually written letter. So we're left with the paradox that letters are used in direct mail because they are the most natural form of personal address in the mailing context, but the experts typically write them in such a way that no one could for a moment mistake them for individually composed letters.

If you use an agency for the creation of your direct mail advertising, follow their advice. But if you're starting out by writing your own direct mail letters, you'll probably do best to try to make them look like ordinary business letters. Leave the four-page folders etc to the experts who know what they're doing. Much better for you to write a good, straightforward letter than a poor imitation of the professional copy-writer's work.

Style. Even when not matching in, avoid such salutations as *Dear Sir/ Madam* which forcibly bring to the reader's attention that he is looking at an impersonal letter. Prefer *Dear Householder* or *Dear Reader* or some other single salutation appropriate to the product you are selling.

Maintain the tone of personal address in the body of your letter by using or implying such words as *you* and *your* whenever possible. Write in a simple and straightforward style, imagining yourself talking about the product to an individual prospect sitting across the table from you.

Let the impact of your letter lie in its ideas and facts, not in any wildness of language. Don't seek to generate an artificial excitement by using exaggerated words like *fantastic*, *incredible* etc or by underlining words or capitalising them for emphasis. Used sparingly, such devices can indeed improve a letter, but the amateur's mistake is to weigh the letter down with such tricks so that every word screams for attention, and the reader, in a daze, simply shuts his mind to the whole thing. Plain, sober, factual English is always to be preferred.

Content. The amount of detail in your letter will depend upon whether it is a *covering letter* only or a more thoroughgoing *sales letter*. A mailshot typically has a number of enclosures in addition to the letter: sales literature, price list, order form etc. The aim of a covering letter is to encourage the reader to approach the accompanying literature in a favourable frame of mind, and to direct his attention to the main substance of the offer. A sales letter, on the other hand, forms a major part of – or even the whole of – the direct mail sales package.

If the mailshot is an attempt at one-stage selling, and so goes to people who haven't specifically asked for it, then you should give your letter a headline, which, just like the headline in a press advertisement, is intended to hook the reader's attention. Put the headline in capital letters on a line by itself just under the salutation.

If the letter is the second stage of a two-stage selling campaign, and so goes to people who have been prompted to write in by your first-stage advertisement, then your letter should tie in with that first-stage advertisement. Just as in the ad itself the sales message had to tie in with the headline, so now the letter must tie in with the ad. If, for example, your ad had invited people to send for details of a new miniature camera, small enough to fit into a typical audio cassette case, then your letter should also stress right at the start the extreme compactness of the camera. *That* was the feature that prompted the enquiries, so *that* is the feature which allows you confidently to engage the enquirer's attention as soon as he starts reading your letter.

Keep in mind the principle of structure as you write your letter, and move coherently from headline to sales message to call to action. If it's a covering letter only, the call to action will be to study the accompanying literature. If it's a sales letter, then its call to action will be as detailed and specific as in an off-the-page sales advertisement.

Construct your letter in a logical order. Having caught the reader's attention with the headline, work on his aroused interest by explaining *how* the product will benefit him by virtue of its unique characteristics. Try to give a series of reasons, supported by factual reference, *why* the product will benefit him. Finally, set out exactly *what* the customer must do next. If you follow your letter through logically in this way, it will hang together as a unit, and will thus have a greater chance of success than any set of random observations.

Don't talk about yourself or your business. Your prospect is not the least bit interested in you, what you think, how you conduct your affairs, or anything else about you. His sole concern is what's in it for him. Bear that in mind, and you should be able to hold his attention.

Pictures

Although the quality of reproduction in the press is improving with the use of new printing technology, in many papers it is still rather poor. Line drawings often reproduce much better than photographs, and can also use a small space more effectively. Match your decision to the particular paper by studying the quality of its printed drawings and photographs.

Every picture tells a story

Consider illustrating your product *in use* as well as in detailed close-up.

The context of use can be an important part of the sales message. If, for example, the picture shows your binoculars being used by someone on a racing yacht looking at a distant buoy, you're implying something about the ruggedness of the product, its waterproof construction and useful power of magnification, even if nothing in the wording mentions any of these matters.

Hidden sales messages

Illustrations can effectively say many things without seeming to be saying them at all. The intangible benefits of your product can be hinted at in ways that reach your prospective customer's understanding without being filtered through his conscious awareness.

Suppose you're selling sunglasses, for example. In classified advertising, there's not a lot you can say really. You can stress their strength, lightness, cheapness, and so on, or invite people to send for your free, beautifully illustrated brochure. The display advertiser, on the other hand, can put an illustration right there on the page, and not only make clear his product's elegance of design, but also show it in whatever real-life context he chooses.

If the illustration shows the glasses being worn by a tennis player smashing an ace into his opponent's court, the hidden sales message is: 'These glasses are good for sporting, energetic types – for people who go out there and *win*.' If the illustration shows an elegant young woman wearing the glasses, walking along a smart shopping boulevard, apparently unaware of the admiring heads turned in her direction as she passes, the hidden sales message is: 'Girls who wear these glasses are beautiful, sophisticated, cool and confident, and can create a minor sensation on a casual stroll.'

The hidden message itself has a subtext: 'Buy our sunglasses, and become one of life's winners' or 'Buy our sunglasses, and be the girl all the men adore and all the women envy.' Turned explicitly into words, the message is crude and unconvincing. Left as a subliminal suggestion in a photograph or drawing, the magic does its work. And potential buyers – probably without realising it and almost certainly without acknowledging it – wishing to identify with the illustrated images, are influenced in their purchasing decisions by the unspoken but alluring promise of worldly success.

Design

Design concerns the way the different components of an advertisement are fitted together to give, normally, a single coherent impression. It has a wider meaning also, not exclusively visual, but still concerning the elegance of fit of the different components of any whole – as, for example, the different enclosures of a mailshot, each of which should support and be supported by the others, all of them together forming an integrated sales package.

There are two things to consider here: the total make-up of your advertisement, looked at on the drawing board, and its appearance in the context in which the reader sees it. Both are equally important.

Here's just one way in which an ad that looks fine on its own can turn out to be a disaster in company. You may, for example, feel very pleased with the amount of useful selling information you have packed into your display ad, listing your various products and prices, one to a line. But if, when published, the ad happens to appear immediately above another, composed of a similar list, the reader wishing to send for one of *your* products may find that his eye travels straight down to the bottom of your competitor's ad in order to find the ordering address. So some sort of border to your advertisement, clearly defining the boundaries of your own sales pitch, is vital, even if you have to make space for it by leaving out some of the sales information you wanted to include. Without a border, all sorts of misfortunes can occur when your advertising copy merges in readers' eyes and minds with that of your competitors.

Order forms

One order form looks much like another, and indeed is. The best way for a beginner to design a form is to look at the forms other advertisers are using, try them out, ie fill in the details asked for so as to test how satisfactory they are, and then model your own form on what looks to you to be the best of the bunch.

Classified advertising

The only visual design opportunities normally available to the classified advertiser are in the choice between **bold type** and ordinary type, and between upper case and lower case letters (ie CAPITALS and non-capitals).

Yet even such limited resources can be exploited creatively. Consider the different impact in a column of print of each of the following:

1. *Old lead toy soldiers, many in original boxes.*
   Free catalogue . . .
2. *OLD LEAD TOY SOLDIERS, MANY IN ORIGINAL BOXES.*
   FREE CATALOGUE . . .
3. *OLD LEAD toy soldiers, MANY IN ORIGINAL BOXES.*

Free catalogue . . .

4. *OLD LEAD TOY SOLDIERS, many in original boxes.*
   FREE catalogue . . .

'On the drawing board' there's nothing to choose between 1 and 2. If the whole ad is set in the same case and typeface, no one word or phrase has any greater typographical impact than the rest, and it is immaterial whether you use upper or lower case, or bold or ordinary type. But within the context of the column, these things may be significant. If most of the column is in ordinary lower case, and your ad uses bold or upper case, then clearly your ad will stand out, though with no typographical variation to point up the sense of what is being said, its impact may still be less than you hoped for.

Example 3 above attempts to make the ad stand out in the column of print by setting the opening words in upper case, and using upper case again to highlight a main selling feature. But it hasn't been done very intelligently. What first catches the reader's eye is *OLD LEAD*, and while this may excite the interest of a scrap metal merchant, it could well miss the collector of old toy soldiers altogether. The next eye-catching phrase MANY IN ORIGINAL BOXES is pretty meaningless unless the attention of the toy soldier collector has already been secured; the eye may be caught but it won't be held.

Example 4 is a much better effort. The typography follows the sense. The whole of the headline *OLD LEAD TOY SOLDIERS* is designed both in meaning and appearance to hook the interest of the target customer, who barely has time to control his excitement at the thought of those tempting *original boxes* before the word *FREE* hits him between the eyes and has him frantically scrabbling for pen and paper to write off for his catalogue before the last post goes. Let's hope so anyway.

Semi-display advertising

The term *semi-display* is sometimes used for advertising, published on classified pages, and normally using the same typefaces as the classified advertising, but giving the advertiser the option to space the wording of his copy. Whereas classified advertising is *set close* – the text running from line to line just as it comes – semi-display can be laid out to your specification, normally set within rules to separate it from the rest of the classified advertising.

You might choose to lay out the tin soldier copy like this:

OLD LEAD TOY SOLDIERS
Many in original boxes.
FREE CATALOGUE
from
. . .

When text is displayed in this way, the line-breaks and the centring or otherwise of the text within the lines make a major contribution to the message. They become additional forms of punctuation, giving the copywriter greater control over the way his message is read and the *pace* at which its component parts are savoured and understood.

These considerations also apply to any form of advertising which uses *display type*, ie large eye-catching lettering as opposed to the *body type* of a continuous piece of prose, set close in the normal way.

Indeed, semi-display advertising is not so much a different form of advertising as a different way of charging for it. Papers that offer it charge for it by the space occupied, in the same way as display advertising, though normally at a lower rate than display advertising which gives you complete typographical, pictorial and design freedom.

Display advertising

A display advertisement is composed of shapes and blank space. Some of the shapes are ready-made and conventional, like the letters of the alphabet; others are representational, like drawings or photographs of your product; others again are abstract, like circles or squares or areas of shading.

The blank space, while in one sense being merely the unprinted parts of the advertising area, is not to be thought of as neutral or wasted or merely the probable background consequence of defining a shape. Blank space can be as positive in its impact as an area of print. One way of ensuring that your small display ad stands out from surroundings advertising is to put your copy within a framework of blank space: wide margins to left, right, top and bottom.

Getting the work done
If you were to instruct a large agency to create your display ad, you might find a small army of experts attacking the problem, including such people as: *the copywriter* to compose the wording, *the visualiser* to produce sketches of the ideas as they progress, *the typographer* to choose typefaces and sizes to match the ideas and fit the available space, *the layout artist* to mark up the finally approved sketch with precise printing instructions,

and possibly others too. They may have different names from those above, as agencies are not at their least creative in the matter of job labels, but these names nevertheless fairly indicate the sort of work that has to be done.

In a small agency, all of the work may be done by one person, and if you use no agency at all, it will have to be: you.

As already suggested, the best option for the new advertiser, short of cash and not himself an accomplished artist, is to do the work of the copywriter and visualiser, and then hand the sketch over to a design studio, either an independent one in your own locality or the design department of the paper in which you propose to advertise, for the finished artwork to be produced.

Designing a display advertisement: a DIY approach

Here's a way of having a go at creating your own display advertising, although the same basic approach can be used for creating advertising leaflets or any other illustrated sales literature.

1. Get a book illustrating different typefaces. Probably the most useful for this and a number of other design purposes is the Letraset catalogue, which describes itself with some justification as a 'graphic design handbook'. Excellent value at £4.99 (1992 price), it illustrates the complete range of Letraset's dry transfer products, some hundreds of typefaces, together with other designs such as symbols, stock illustrations, shades, lines, borders and geometric shapes. It also has details of various drawing and design aids, which you will at least find useful to know about, and – depending on your degree of enthusiasm – may wish to buy. You can get a copy of the Letraset catalogue from shops specialising in drawing equipment and artists' supplies.

2. If you are intending to use colour, a special colour specifier is useful. This enables you to choose precise shades and name them unambiguously when dealing with printers or professional designers. The Pantone system is widely used for this purpose. It provides several hundred standard colours, each with its own reference number. This enables a designer to say to a printer that the colour required in a particular place is, for example, Pantone 469, and the printer will know precisely the colour meant. This is plainly more helpful than saying that what you want is a sort of darkish brown. Reference sets of Pantone colours are readily available. The Letraset catalogue has details of a number of them, and does itself include a helpful reference colour chart.

3. Get yourself a good supply of blank paper, not smaller than A4,

and some well sharpened pencils. Also ruler, eraser, sharpener etc. A desktop publishing (DTP) program run on a personal computer can be a useful additional aid here. DTP programs are available for all the popular computer systems and cost roughly £100 upwards (1992 prices). If you already use a computer in your business, check the advertisements in computer journals for details of currently available DTP programs.

4. You will probably find it easier to work out your ideas on a large scale irrespective of the size of the ad. Precisely measure the intended advertising space, and draw a large frame which maintains the same proportions of height to width, so that you know your work can be ultimately scaled to the right size.

5. From time to time as you work, try out your ideas on an actual-size advertising space. Making a design fit a given space cannot always be effectively achieved merely by scaling up or down. Some things that work in a large space may look fussy, cramped or even unreadable in a small one.

6. Remember the three-part structure of an ad: headline, sales message, call to action. Tackle each part separately, giving each its due weight and importance.

7. Start with the sales message. This is the heart of any advertisement. Draw up two lists of the attributes of your product. In List A, write down all the *facts*: the objectively verifiable specification of the product: size, weight, price etc. In List B, write down all the *benefits* the product offers the purchaser: saves him money, improves his appearance, increases his confidence etc.

8. Study Lists A and B above and decide precisely which of these facts and benefits you want your sales message to include. You almost certainly won't have space to put in everything. Select a single feature to which your advertisement will give greatest prominence, and decide which other features you will refer to as subsidiary and supporting arguments in your sales presentation.

9. Sketch out the sales message. Words only? Words and picture(s)? Picture(s) only? No need to be too detailed at this stage. Just block in some ideas on your paper – a rough placing and idea for the illustration, if any, with the space allotted to the body type of the sales message.

10. Work out a headline. It should be short and punchy. The casual looker-on – someone not consciously reading but merely looking at the page – must be able to take in the headline at a glance. Remember to target the headline at the sort of person likely to be interested in your sales message.

11. Think about typeface, size and display of your headline. Refer to

your book of typefaces and experiment with different ideas. Consider the different effects that different styles and layouts will achieve.

12. Block your headline in roughly on your draft, and start thinking how it will dovetail with your sales message both in meaning and design. Keep sketching your ideas out on paper.

13. Don't be mean with the stationery. The more ideas you can get down on paper, the better. You almost certainly won't finish your work at a single sitting. When you come back to your drawing board tomorrow, you'll be grateful for all the half-formed and even half-baked ideas preserved in your sketches, along with the sudden shafts of inspiration, though by tomorrow they may not seem all that inspired. In any creative exercise the greatest difficulty is in getting started, writing or drawing the first useful mark on that intimidatingly blank sheet of paper. Even poor and plainly unsuitable sketches can help to prime the inspirational pump. The thing is to keep the ideas coming, and not to reject in your mind too many thoughts merely because they seem less than perfect. Get them down on paper. With any luck, sooner or later the ideas will seem to come out at you *from* the paper; they are unlikely to spring pre-formed and perfect straight out of your head.

14. Work out the call to action. Will it include a reply coupon? If so, how much space will it need? Check out the practicalities on your actual-size draft.

15. Rough out the whole thing again. Apart from the headline, don't bother with specific wording or detailed drawing. Just block out what goes where, and satisfy yourself that it balances well – not too much print, not too much empty space. Do the headline, sales message and call to action each occupy an appropriate amount of the design for the things you intend to say and the effect you wish to create?

16. Are the boundaries of your advertising space well defined, so that there is no risk that the reader's eye will drift out of your space into that of a neighbouring advertiser?

17. Once you are satisfied with your rough design, start working on the detail of the content. Compose the text of your sales message, once again bearing in mind the different effects that typeface, size, punctuation and line-breaks can give. Constantly check with the actual-size draft that there is enough room to accommodate the proposed text.

18. Sketch in the main outline of any drawing or photograph included in your design.

19. Produce your final draft, and label it as necessary with details of the typefaces and, if appropriate, the colours to be used. If you have any finished drawings or photographs which are to be included in the advertisement, keep these separate from your draft, merely sketching it on the draft where they are to appear.

20. Take your final effort, plus any separate drawings or photographs, along to a design studio and ask them to prepare finished artwork on the basis of your ideas. If possible, sit down with the designer and discuss your ideas and consider any suggestions he has to make.

21. You or the studio will have to check with the paper in which you intend to advertise to see in what form and in exactly what dimensions they require advertising copy. Major advertisers normally supply their artwork in the form of film run off a computer disk. However, *camera ready copy* – ie the original artwork, which the paper publishers can process themselves – is generally acceptable.

22. Whether the paper's technology is ancient or modern, you will be able to leave space in your copy for textual amendments to be made for any particular publication of your advertisement. For example, you will probably want to change the key (see page 139) each time the advertisement is published, and you may also want to allow yourself the option of changing, say, the displayed price of the product or p&p charge, or even the wording of the call to action. If the changes are purely textual, they are easily made when required.

Study the practitioners

And now here's something you can do right away to advance your understanding of the creation and design of mail order advertisements. Pick up any paper or magazine with mail order advertising in it, or the contents of any mailshot that's come through your door, and try to analyse the advertisers' techniques: what they're doing, how they're doing it, and how effectively.

This isn't a once-only exercise. The analysis of other people's advertising is something you can and should continue to do throughout your mail order career.

Although you can work at this sort of exercise by yourself, you'll find you get the greatest value from it if you work with one or two others. Discussing views, problems and suggestions with other interested people is an excellent way of sorting out your own ideas and familiarising yourself with the nuts and bolts of ad construction.

Choose a piece of mail order advertising copy and, using the following list of comments and questions to prompt your thinking or discussion, try to see what it aims to do, how it's been put together and how well you think it works. Three warnings before you start:

1. The list is not exhaustive – it's just to help you get started.
2. Not all questions apply to all forms of advertising.
3. No amount of analysis of this kind will reveal whether an advertisement is *successful* – ie makes money.

As pointed out elsewhere, an advertisement is just the visible tip of the advertising campaign iceberg; here, all you're considering is that fraction of the whole. Be on your guard against the sort of complacent wrongheadedness exemplified by the surgeon who came out of the theatre to report delightedly that the operation had been a total success though regrettably the patient had died.

1. Identify the headline, the sales message, the call to action, the key.
2. Is the headline eye-catching? Whose eye is it designed to catch? In your view, has the advertiser got it right – that is, will the headline attract the maximum number of potential customers, those likely to be interested in the sales message, and ultimately in buying the product?
3. In your view, who are the likely customers for the product? On the basis of the advertisement copy, who do you think the advertiser believes to be his likely customers?
4. Read the sales message as if you were a genuine potential customer. Is it clear? Persuasive? Does it hold your interest? Why? Or why not?
5. Does the advertiser stress the factual specification of the product? Or its benefits? Or both? Or neither?
6. How effective are the illustrations, if any? Are they merely decorative or are they an effective part of the sales message? Are they saying, 'This is what the product looks like' or are they additionally saying, 'This is what the product does and what its benefits are'?
7. Are there any hidden sales messages?
8. How effectively are different typefaces and sizes used?
9. Does the layout of the text – line-breaks, centring etc – contribute to its effect?
10. How effective is the call to action? Is it clear? Does the advertiser use any inducements to prompt immediate action?
11. If a mailshot, how clear or confusing is the relationship between the different enclosures?

12. How many different things must the reader do in order to accept the advertised offer?
13. How is the price expressed? Post free? P&p extra?
14. Is the boundary of the advertising space clear, or does it tend to merge into the surrounding advertisements?
15. How well does the advertisement stand out from the other print and pictures on the page?
16. Do you think the advertisement could be improved? How?

Chapter 9

Advertising in the Press

We saw in Chapter 5 that you may have hurdles to jump if you wish to advertise in the press. The hurdles are likely to be higher and trickier for display advertising than for classified, for off-the-page selling than for two-stage selling, and for the major national papers than for the minor, though still national, periodicals. But hurdles are there to be jumped, and you either jump them or you're out of the race.

In the present chapter we look at the mechanics of press advertising for those still in the running.

Rate cards

Papers set out their advertising charges on *rate cards*, which normally distinguish three main types of advertising: space advertising, classified advertising, and inserts.

Space advertising

Space advertising, which comprises both display and semi-display, is charged for by the size of space occupied. There are various ways in which sizes are typically expressed. You may meet any of the following:

1. Page fractions, eg whole page, half page, one-sixth page etc;
2. Single column centimetres (scc), eg *10 scc* is a space 10 centimetres deep and 1 column wide;
3. Depth by numbers of columns, eg *135mm × 4* is a space 135 millimetres deep and 4 columns wide;
4. Depth by width, eg *135 × 175mm* is a space 135 millimetres deep and 175 millimetres wide.

Watch out for the confusing mixture of centimetres and millimetres. Rate cards favour whole numbers, and there is a tendency to keep to centimetres for as long as possible but to slip into millimetres when fractions threaten.

The typical mail order bargain square is 4 scc or 5 scc.

When does 5 scc not equal 5 scc?
Regrettably often. While a centimetre is the same for everybody, page

132

sizes and column widths vary from paper to paper; indeed, column widths frequently vary from page to page within the same paper. This lack of standardisation causes problems. A piece of artwork that is a perfect fit for 5 scc in one paper may be cramped into illegibility in what is nominally the same space in another paper. Size variations of this kind also help to confuse cost comparisons between different papers.

Get a ruler or scissors and investigate some papers for yourself. Measure or cut out one or two mail order ads from one paper and try to position them in the columns of another. See what the implications are for space and cost. Would a straight scaling up or down allow the ads of one paper to fit the columns of another? Or would this lead either to cramping or to unwanted blank space at top and bottom or at the sides? Since a single column centimetre can cost over £100 in some papers, the considerations are clearly more than just aesthetic.

Classified advertising

Different papers define classified advertising differently. In some papers even display advertising is regarded as classified if it appears under a specific heading. This, by the way, has implications for the various MOPS since some of them exclude classified advertising from their protection.

Here, however, we use the term *classified advertising* as it is commonly understood by the general public: an ad consisting of words only, the text running on from line to line in uniform body type, and appearing under a heading provided by the paper.

Classified advertising is charged either as *linage* or *wordage*, ie either by the line or by the word.

Although for any given paper you have no choice in the matter, wordage is the more satisfactory system as it allows you to plan your advertising costs precisely. With linage you have to try to estimate how many lines of print your copy will run to, and some papers seem unnecessarily generous with *their* space and *your* money. If you are paying, say, £12 a line, it is a little annoying to find that the printer has so widely spaced your wording that you just spill over into a fifth line and so have a bill for £60 instead of £48. That additional 25 per cent of advertising money could easily represent the difference between success and failure.

If you suspect that you may be the victim of needlessly wide spacing – and it is easy to check a paper in advance to see what their usual practice is – you should stipulate the maximum number of lines in which you ad is to be set. Make it a condition of your order. If you are told that the ad won't fit your limited number of lines, you have at least the choice of paying more or not advertising at all. Budgetary control will not have been taken out of your hands.

Inserts

Most papers will accept your own advertising leaflets and either slip them in loose or bind them into the publication. You supply the ready-printed leaflets, the paper charging you a rate per thousand for inserting them. Though there is normally a minimum number they will accept – say, 15,000 or 25,000 – you're not obliged to provide leaflets for the complete print run of the paper.

Finding out about press advertising

If you use an agency, they will be able to advise you on suitable papers, cost, and everything else. If you're on your own, you have to do your own research.

You can always get all the information you need by direct enquiry to the papers of your choice. Ask them for their rate cards. But it may be helpful at first to have a broad spread of information available in one place, so that you can see which papers specialise in which areas, what their advertising rates are, their circulation figures, and how one publication compares with another.

British Rate and Data (BRAD)

BRAD contains full up-to-date advertising information on virtually all papers and periodicals in the UK: advertising rates, circulation figures, notice required for placing or cancelling advertising, and *mechanical* data, ie printing specifications such as column width, page size, the form in which artwork must be submitted, and so on. Also useful for elementary research is its classified arrangement which brings together journals covering similar areas of interest.

BRAD, published monthly, is available on subscription for £325 a year; single copies cost £130 each (1992 prices). Yes, that does say one hundred and thirty pounds each – how about that as a way of deterring the frivolous! If you use an advertising agency, they will certainly have *BRAD* available. (Why not see if you can scrounge last month's copy from them?) If you're on your own, you should be able to find a public reference library somewhere within reach which subscribes to *BRAD* – your local librarian will know where the nearest one is. It is well worth going out of your way to see what *BRAD* has to offer. There is no other publication so packed with up-to-date information about the advertising media.

Advertisers Annual
Published annually in December, *Advertisers Annual* has, among other things, an extensive classified listing of UK papers and periodicals with a brief indication of advertising rates – enough, at least, to allow a first comparison of rates between different publications. It also gives circulation figures and a brief amount of mechanical data. With any luck, your local library should have a copy of either *Advertisers Annual* or of the guide below.

Willing's Press Guide
Published annually in February, *Willing's Press Guide* includes basic information about UK papers and periodicals, classified listings, circulation figures etc. It does not include advertising rates or mechanical data.

Where to advertise

Study over a period the papers you think would suit your advertising. What you are looking for are places where other mail order dealers in similar products to your own are regularly advertising: these are your active mail order markets. Don't waste your money advertising anywhere else.

Advertising rates

Advertising rates vary enormously from paper to paper. Here are some typical examples, at 1992 rates, of the cost (before VAT) of mail order bargain squares: *Daily Express* £425, *Daily Mirror* £475, *Daily Telegraph* £250, the *Sun* £425, *Sunday Telegraph* £200, *Sunday People* £370, *News of the World* £550, *Time Out* £102.50, *The Lady* £78, *DIY Magazine* £118.

If you're thinking of taking a full page, typical costs could be: *Radio Times* £14,000 (or £19,000 for colour), the *Sun* £28,000 (rates vary over the week), *Sunday Times Magazine* £11,000 (or £16,000 for colour), *Amateur Photographer* £1050 (or £2090 for colour). Smaller spaces are broadly proportionate in cost.

Classified advertising rates range from pence per word to pounds per line. You will often find the rates indicated somewhere on the advertising pages themselves.

Circulation and readership

The main reason for such huge variations in cost is *circulation*, ie the average number of copies sold per issue. Clearly, a paper with a

135

circulation of a million offers more to its advertisers than a paper with a circulation of half a million.

But circulation is only part of the story. Two papers with the same circulation figures may have very different *readership* figures, ie the total number of people who have the opportunity to read each issue. A popular daily delivered to a typical household may be read by mother, father, son and daughter; a specialist periodical may only be read by the person who buys it.

Where do these figures come from?

Any paper's claimed circulation or readership should be taken with a pinch of salt unless there is some independent verification. Fortunately, there often is. There are two independent bodies which by monitoring and research authenticate the figures. These are the Audit Bureau of Circulations (ABC) and the Joint Industry Committee for National Readership Surveys (JICNARS). Both bodies produce updated figures half-yearly. You can confidently accept the accuracy of any ABC circulation figures or any JICNARS readership figures. Papers which can quote such independent verification normally cite ABC and JICNARS (or NRS - see below) in their published claims.

Readership profile

In its National Readership Surveys (NRS), JICNARS uses a system of social grading which classifies people by reference to the occupation of the head of the household. Grades A, B and C1 are respectively top, middle and junior managers and corresponding levels of professional people and administrators. Grades C2 and D are respectively skilled and semi-skilled/unskilled manual workers. Grade E is everyone else - the unemployed, the retired etc.

Though based upon the jobs people do, the grades are also assumed to imply something about social attitudes, life-styles and purchasing power, hence their value to the advertiser. If you're selling a product that would interest owners of private aircraft, it would make sense for you to look for a paper with a high percentage of grade A readers; if your product is designed for bingo enthusiasts, you should probably be looking for a large C2/D readership.

Grades are often bracketed together to simplify the profile. For example, in 1992 *The Lady* described its class readership as 27 per cent AB, 35 per cent C1, 19 per cent C2 and 19 per cent DE.

Value for money

One way of comparing one paper's value with another is to express the advertising rates in terms of the cost per thousand readers. If your ad in paper X, with a readership of 4 million, costs £500, while in paper Y, with a readership of 2 million, it costs £300, then, on the face of it, you're getting better value from the former: 1000 readers cost you 15p in Y but only 12.5p in X.

Although this is a calculation always worth making, it is very difficult to know how much significance to attach to it. Plainly, readership *profile* is crucially important, and must at least be considered in conjunction with the raw readership figures. A paper read by a few thousand mail-order-mad millionaires would obviously suit you better than one read by a few million penniless semi-literates, whatever the rates.

Don't be dazzled by large circulation figures or low cost per thousand readers. Take these things into account, of course, but remember that your aim is to target your advertising so that it reaches the greatest number of people who are seriously likely to be interested in your product, and willing and able to buy it. No matter how low the advertising rate, it's still too high if the readers aren't in your market.

Positioning your advertisement

Choosing the right position for your ad within a paper may be as important as choosing the right paper in the first place.

Classified advertising

With a classified ad, your only choice about position is which column it should go into. Yet even this seemingly straightforward choice is worth some thought.

Suppose, for example, you are selling an anti-rust compound for use on cars. The obvious place for your ad would be the Motor Accessories column. But you might feel that people give more thought to the maintenance of their cars immediately they have bought them, as this is the time when even the most undedicated motorist is briefly enthusiastic. So why not run your ad in the Cars for Sale column, aiming to reach those who might, just at this time, be responsive to your message and act upon it as soon as they have found a car to buy?

The right place to advertise is not where your customers expect to find *you*, but where you expect to find your customers.

Display advertising

If the paper has a special mail order section called 'Postal Bargains' or something similar, then this is probably where you will want your ad to go. If there is no mail order section, and you give no special instruction, the paper will treat it as a *run of paper* (ROP) ad, ie it will be fitted in wherever there happens to be room. So your offer of ladies' underwear could find itself tucked away at the bottom of the city page, or your offer of a businessman's diary might be slotted into a page otherwise devoted to teenage fashions.

Such disasters are avoidable if you specify where your ad is to appear, though to do so will usually cost you a premium over the basic advertising rate. The broadest specification is *facing matter* (or *next matter*) which means next to editorial material, not on a purely advertising page. Other fairly standard options are for the front page or back page, book page, TV page, facing correspondence, and so on. Righthand pages may cost more than lefthand pages, and a top righthand corner more than a position within the page. *Solus* positions can be specified, ie the only ad on an editorial page.

When considering these options, keep in mind the general principle that the best place to be is where the other mail order ads of similar products are. And if there are no such ads, then you probably shouldn't be there either.

A/B split runs

Some papers offer a copy testing facility which allows you to vary a feature of your ad. Versions A and B of the ad are printed in alternate copies of the same issue of the paper. So, for example, A might use an ordinary address while B uses a Freepost address; or A might offer a free gift with the product while B doesn't. Such A/B split runs are the ideal way of testing particular features of a press ad because they entirely eliminate the uncertainties which characterise copy testing in successive issues of a paper.

If, for example, you ran one version of your ad last week, and the alternative version this week, there is always the possibility that any difference in the results has been caused by factors unrelated to the ad itself. Perhaps the weather has changed markedly, or some major event is dominating public thinking this week, or the position of the ad within the paper is different, or last week there were competing advertisers and this week there are not, or last week the paper carried a story which had a direct and favourable bearing upon your ad and this week it doesn't, and so on. The possibilities are limitless, unpredictable, imponderable and outside your control. And all of them are removed by using the A/B split facility, since precisely the same external factors operate upon both versions and therefore cancel out.

Frequency

Because of the external imponderables referred to above, no single insertion of an ad can give you a reliable measure of its worth. You will need to run it at least three or four times in consecutive issues to smooth out the variations.

Keys

It is important to be able to attribute the replies you receive to the particular ads that prompted them so that you can analyse your results and modify your advertising accordingly. If your ad includes a coupon, you can ensure that it has a reference code printed on it, eg *EM/19.3.92* would tell you immediately that the coupon comes from your ad in *Exchange & Mart* on 19 March 1992. Such reference codes are known as *keys*.

If you're not using a coupon ad, then you should put a key in your published address, eg *Send your order to Mailmagic (Dept DM/3), 77 High Street . . .*, the Dept number being the reference code identifying your ad no 3 in the *Daily Mirror*. Incorporating the key in your address has the added advantage of allowing you to sort the mail even before you open the envelopes.

Without keys, it is impossible to calculate the success or failure of particular ads for the same product. Suppose that the time has come when you are publishing your advertising in six different papers. It may be that by lumping the results together in your calculations, you are clearly making a profit. But a more detailed examination may reveal that while four of the ads are doing very well, one consistently fails to break even, and the final one never attracts a single order. Without the information the keys provide, you would continue wasting money on the two losers simply because your overall level of success is high enough to disguise their failure.

Alternatively, it may be that your six ads, lumped together, show a steady loss, entirely due to one or two concealed losers. Identify and cancel the losing ads, and you convert a steady loss into a steady profit.

Paying for your advertising

Unless you are placing your advertising through a recognised agency, you will probably at first have to pay for it in advance. If you become a regular advertiser, however, try to open accounts with papers you regularly use. Credit from the media helps your cash flow position; particularly if you are selling off the page, your advertising will generate income before the bills for it fall due.

The life of an advertisement

The life of an ad depends upon the life of the paper it is published in. Most publications are retained by the reader until the next issue appears. Some periodicals, particularly ones of specialist interest, may be kept much longer or even filed away permanently.

Advertisements are like old soldiers that don't die but just fade away. When you have been in business for a length of time, you will become used to getting the odd reply now and then from an ad published months or even years before, possibly from a remote part of the world where the paper may have been lovingly preserved as a memento of Britain, or more prosaically done service as a drawer liner. While these things stir the imagination, they don't do much for business, and for all practical purposes you can consider that an ad in a daily paper will have produced all its replies within a week, a weekly within three weeks, and a monthly within three months. In all cases, about two-thirds of the replies will come within about the first third of the total period. Assume that an ad is clinically dead when a week elapses without further replies.

Chapter 10

Direct Mail

In one way – though in one way only – direct mail is much easier for the beginner than press advertising. It's easier because you can get going without first needing to satisfy anyone of your financial standing, business bona fides, stock position or anything else. You can post your sales message in a letter-box just as easily as you can post a letter to a friend. Even if the press are putting insuperable obstacles in the way of your advertising, the post is still open to you, and it's far from being a second-rate option. Figures available from the Direct Mail Information Service show that direct mail is the UK's third largest advertising medium, after the press and television, accounting in 1990 for £979 million of advertising expenditure.

One similarity between direct mail and press advertising is that most of the people addressed fail to respond. But in direct mail, even a negative response requires a positive action – the recipient actually has to throw the mailshot away – whereas an ad in the paper can simply be ignored, the reader often remaining unaware that he *has* ignored it.

This need to take *some* action when you find a mailshot in your post is one of direct mail's strengths. Whatever the critics of direct mail may profess, it's very difficult indeed to throw a letter away unopened – have *you* ever done it? Most people at least take a quick peek inside the envelope, and some of those who do so then have their attention caught, and a fraction of *those* go on to accept the offer. The acceptances, even for a successful mailing, may be no more than two people in every 100 – which at first sounds pitiful. But if the press advertisers canvassed by Dave Patten had done as 'pitifully' (see page 27), then instead of each averaging 10 sales to the 3 million readership, they would each have averaged 60,000 sales!

Profits

We saw on page 28 that a fairly typical direct mail operation with a rented list might cost you £350 for 1000 mailshots – £180 postage, £100 enclosures, £70 rental. A 2 per cent *conversion*, ie the number of sales as a percentage of the number of mailshots, means that you make 20 sales, each of which has therefore cost you £17.50. The implications of that are not difficult to see. If your gross profit per sale averages less than £17.50, you lose money; if it averages more than £17.50, you make money.

But suppose you could do better than 2 per cent, what then? And what if you use your own list instead of renting one at £70. Here is a table showing the approximate cost to you per sale for different conversion rates, assuming a basic post-&-enclosures cost of £280 and a rental fee, if applicable, of £70:

Conversion	No of sales per thousand	Cost per sale (rented list)	Cost per sale (own list)
2%	20	£17.50	£14.00
3%	30	£11.67	£9.33
4%	40	£8.75	£7.00
5%	50	£7.00	£5.60
6%	60	£5.83	£4.67
7%	70	£5.00	£4.00
8%	80	£4.38	£3.50
9%	90	£3.89	£3.11
10%	100	£3.50	£2.80

You can see that at the lower conversions even a 1 per cent improvement makes an enormous difference. Suppose you're selling your product at a gross profit of £14. A 2 per cent conversion with the rented list loses you £3.50 per sale – a loss of £70 for every 1000 mailshots. The same conversion with your own list, and you break even. A 3 per cent rate with the rented list, and you earn £2.33 per sale – £70 for your 30 sales to 1000 people; and the same rate with your own list doubles your profit to £140.

The above calculations have been simplified to illustrate the point that seemingly marginal changes to the underlying figures can produce startling differences to the profit and loss account. In practice, all sorts of other variables play their part. For example, even if you use your own list, you may have labelling costs. Even if you use a rented list, it may cost you more or less than £70. Your enclosures may similarly come to more or less than £100. And if your total mailing is large enough, you may qualify for a Mailsort rebate which, at 1992 prices, could reduce your postage per 1000 from £180 to about £150.

The moral, however, is clear. In large mailings, the smallest improvement can have a decisive effect upon the final figures.

Mailing lists

The quality of the mailing list you use is of paramount importance, and the quality looked for is twofold. The list must be good in itself – well constructed and well maintained – and it must have the right profile for your purpose.

Construction

A list is constructed either by research or as the by-product of some other activity. Construction determines who goes on the list and who doesn't. The list compiler must have a clear set of criteria to which every name on the list must conform. A well constructed list ruthlessly excludes all other names.

Researched lists

Research is often a matter of combing through existing lists in order to select from them people with the desired characteristics. Suppose you sell a personal security device of particular interest to people who live on their own. One way of constructing a prospect list would be to consult the electoral roll, the annually published list of everyone in the country entitled to vote at parliamentary elections. Since the electoral roll gives addresses, together with the names of eligible voters at each address, you could create your list by noting those addresses at which there was only a single voter. The method wouldn't be foolproof, as it would also, for example, pick households where there was indeed only a single eligible voter but also one or more children – though possibly you would consider such households also to be prime targets for your product.

Perhaps your product will only work in conjunction with the telephone. In that case, you could use the electoral roll to produce a provisional list, from which you remove people without phones by checking for entries in the telephone directory.

Most research is time-consuming and expensive to undertake or to have undertaken on your behalf. The quality of a researched list normally depends upon the ingenuity, thoroughness and meticulousness of the researcher.

Two-stage selling. Though not normally thought of as such, two-stage selling is really a special kind of direct mail. Stage one, pulling in the enquiries, is the research method by which you compile the list to which you mail the full details of your offer. In the nature of the thing, an enquiry list of this kind is very reliable indeed, and the people on it self-selected and therefore positively wishing to be mailed.

The value of the enquiry list for later mailings is much more doubtful, and it is generally not a good idea to merge enquirers and customers into a single list unless the two groups can be segmented (see page 144).

By-product lists

These lists are not constructed to be mailing lists, but come about as the incidental result of some other activity. The construction is often of very

143

high quality as no one has had to justify the cost of compilation by reference to ultimately expected sales.

The electoral roll is this kind of list. Others include membership lists of different organisations, the share registers of public companies, lists of people with particular academic or professional qualifications, and, above all, the customer lists of commercial organisations. Notice it is only the quality of *construction* we're talking of here. If you want a mailing list of deaf-aid wearers, for example, you couldn't get a better constructed list than one composed of the names and addresses of people who have actually bought them. But the same list could be very poor in other respects – if, for example, it hasn't been updated for 10 years.

The best constructed list of all is your own customer list, the by-product of your sales successes. There is something particularly satisfying about acquiring a valuable mailing list as the by-product of a successful sales operation. Herein lies the evolutionary secret of profitable mail order – success breeding success.

Segmentation

Computerisation allows lists to be easily segmented. A *segment* is a subset of the main list. Consider, for example, a list of mail order purchasers of computer software. In addition to the names and addresses, each entry on the list can be coded to show, for example, whether the customer has bought games, utilities or business applications; whether his purchases have been under £30 in value or over £30; whether he has bought once only or more than once; whether he is indeed 'he' or 'she'; his age group; and so on. Some of this information becomes automatically available to the list compiler from the orders received; some of it has to be actively researched, perhaps by asking customers to fill in brief questionnaires.

However it's done, the list's value to the user is now enhanced. If he wants to promote, say, a new accounting package at £60, he can select precisely the segment of the list that looks most promising; purchasers of business applications who spend over £30. By eliminating the rest of the list, he may lose the odd sale or two, but he is almost certain to gain on balance by not wasting money mailing to the mass of the list who were never in the market for the new product. Yet at other times – say, when mailing his autumn catalogue – he can use the complete list.

A segmented list is really a composite of a number of lists, except that no name has to be stored more than once, no matter how many segments it features in.

Maintenance

Maintaining a list, also known as *cleaning* it, involves checking for and deleting double entries, correcting errors, updating listed details as

144

customers move house or change their names, and removing from the list the names of people who have died, or who have indicated that they do not wish to receive further mailings, or who have made no positive response to mailings despatched over an extended period. A rented list on which deads, duds and duplicates have been allowed to collect will lose you money three times over: paying a rental for non-existent customers, paying production costs for the literature you send them, and paying postage to mail it to them.

Duplicates
Most lists of any size are held on computers, and *deduplication* – ugly jargon for the valuable exercise of removing duplicate entries and consolidating their information in one place – is very easily performed.

Non-computerised lists are much more difficult to check for duplicates, and indeed the work can only be done at all if list entries are filed by name or address, and an alert checker laboriously compares each record with its neighbour. Furthermore, additions to an existing list have to be correctly inserted to confirm that the entry is not already present. The work is tedious, time-consuming and costly, perhaps even more costly than leaving the duplicates in place.

Errors
Some errors can be spotted by proofreading entries before finally committing them to the list. An address with 'Strafford-on-Avon' as its post town or 'Mr John Qmith' as the customer will alert the proofreader to check the original order. Other errors – the wrong house number, for example – may be quite unspottable unless detailed comparisons are made of every entry with every order. Postcodes can be checked – or supplied if missing – from directories. The Post Office provides a postcoding service in which it will accept a computerised list on magnetic tape and add the correct postcodes by matching entries with those on its *Postcode Address File*, a regularly updated computer file containing all addresses in the country.

Updating
This is the most important maintenance exercise of all. For one reason or another – death, removal etc – you can typically expect about 12 per cent of any list to be out-of-date within a year. That means, for example, that on a six-year-old list, almost every second name is a dud. Even if you achieve a satisfactory 3 per cent conversion of the active names on such a list, the inactive ones bring your overall conversion down to 1.5 per cent, and that, on the basis of the figures used earlier, would produce a decided operating loss. How galling to be such a good salesman and yet

145

to end up broke because you keep knocking on the doors of empty houses!

There are two things to note here. First, it doesn't matter when the list was originally constructed nor how long any of the names have been on it; the important date for the user is when it was last properly cleaned. A two-year-old list, last used and cleaned six months ago, is almost as good as a list only six months old (only *almost* because inactive names are bound to be accumulating though it's too early to identify them – see *non-buyers* below).

Second, even an old and uncleaned list may still be worth using if it's the best you can find and your gross profit per item sold and your expected conversion rate are sufficiently high. If, for example, a mailing costs you £350 per 1000 and you have reason to suspect that half the names on the list are useless, your effective cost per 1000 becomes £700. But even that won't matter if you can pull in gross profits of *more* than £700 from the list as a whole. Never favour or reject a sales opportunity on general principles: always do the sums.

Post Office returns. The most effective way to clean a list is to ensure that the Post Office returns to you all undeliverable items – *nixies* or *gone aways* in the jargon – every time you use the list. This service costs you nothing; provided you put a return address on your envelopes, nixies come back automatically, and you can then remove the useless names from your list.

So vital is this aspect of list cleaning that the recommended industry practice is for list owners to refund to renters of customer lists the postage on all nixies in excess of 5 per cent of the mailing.

Non-buyers. Even if the mailshot gets delivered, the customer may have lost interest. Decide how long it's worth keeping him on the list if he doesn't buy anything. This will vary from product to product, but three years is probably a reasonable average. Perhaps when the time limit is up, you could enclose with the final mailshot a reply slip for the non-ordering customer to use if he wants to remain on your mailing list. In the absence of orders or reply slips from the oldies on your list, delete them.

Profile

Your own customer list, by definition, is composed of precisely the kind of people who buy your kind of product. If you're thinking of renting someone else's list, you will be looking for a profile that matches your own as closely as possible. If you're just starting out and haven't got a customer list at all, you will have to guess at the profile of your target customers and look for lists that match your guess.

This is sometimes straightforward, sometimes less so. If you're selling books on tennis, a list of existing purchasers of books on tennis would obviously be ideal. But what about purchasers of tennis equipment? Or sports books in general? Or outdoor games equipment in general? Or leisure books? Or just books? While you would prefer an ideal matching, such a list may not exist, and it will be a matter first of guessing and then of testing to see whether a list with a less than ideal profile is worth using.

Geodemographics

Geodemographic systems relate population characteristics to geographical areas. Based on data such as government census statistics and the electoral roll, and using modern high-powered computer technology, systems have been developed which can identify particular areas or particular lists of people as prime targets for particular types of consumer promotion. The rationale of such systems is that people of a given neighbourhood or living in property of a certain type will tend to have tastes, life-style and purchasing habits in common. Though not designed exclusively for the direct mail industry, they are of considerable value to anyone concerned with direct mail or house-to-house distribution.

A number of such systems are operated by companies whose services are commercially available to direct mail users. The DMIS or DMSSB will be able to point you in the direction of suitable agencies.

An example of one of the major geodemographic classification systems is ACORN (A Classification of Residential Neighbourhoods), developed by CACI. The system allows consumers to be classified into varying socio-economic types, according to their residential area.

ACORN recognises 11 main neighbourhood groups: (a) agricultural areas, (b) modern family housing, higher incomes, (c) older housing of intermediate status, (d) older terraced housing, (e) better-off council estates, (f) less well-off council estates, (g) poorest council estates, (h) mixed inner metropolitan areas, (i) high status non-family areas, (j) affluent suburban housing, (k) better-off retirement areas. These main groups are further subdivided to produce a total of 38 neighbourhood types.

ACORN classification is particularly effective when used in conjunction with the results of market research, such as the Target Group Index (TGI), for example, published annually by the British Market Research Bureau. The TGI provides information on over 400 consumer product fields (from food to finance) and some 3500 different named brands. The responses to the TGI are coded by ACORN so that for any product covered in the survey, the ACORN types which show above average usage are identified. Once established, these ACORN types can be used as a tool to reveal which localities offer prime markets for such products.

The ACORN types can also be applied to mailing lists and the electoral rolls in order to identify lists of new customer prospects.

CACI publishes a free booklet *The Acorn User Guide* which lists and describes all the ACORN types and explains in more detail how ACORN can be used.

Choosing a list

There are three types of list to choose from: your own customer list, a researched list, a rented list.

Customer list

As frequently said, your own customer list ought always to give you the best results. Of course, a list is only a mailing list if it exists in a usable form. Going back to the old order documents to retrieve names and addresses every time you want to direct mail your customers, or even rent your list to other users, is not seriously practicable. As soon as you have a file of a few hundred customers, look into the possibility of computerising it. As we have seen, this greatly simplifies list maintenance and segmentation, and also provides the database from which error-free address labels may be speedily printed.

You can get your list on to computer via one of the mailing houses offering list management, or you can deal directly with a computer bureau, or, of course, you can do the work in-house.

Researched lists

Existing lists are almost always cheaper and easier to come by than researched lists. Before embarking on research yourself or instructing someone else to do so, check to see if a list with the right profile and quality does not already exist. Contact a list broker for help with this one. Find addresses in the DMSSB *Handbook*.

Rented lists

Lists are normally rented for one mailing only, at a rental of anything from £50 upwards per 1000 names. £70 or £80 is fairly typical, but rentals over £100 are not uncommon.

Most owners supply their lists ready-printed on self-adhesive labels, but it is almost always possible to have them supplied in some other form, eg on magnetic tape. The advantage of magnetic tape is that it makes possible the checking for names already on your own computerised list.

However the list is supplied, you may only use it once unless you and the owner have made some other special arrangement. Of course, anyone on the list who becomes your customer is legitimately added to your own customer list; but if you want to mail the non-buyers again, you will need to rent the list a second time and pay a second rental.

The list owner will normally ask to see the mailing piece you propose to send before agreeing to rent you his list. The *mailing piece* is the total set of enclosures you propose to mail to each person on the list.

Finding

The best way to find a suitable list to rent is to consult a list broker. As the typical broker's commission of 20 per cent of the list rental is paid by the list owner, there is probably no saving to be made by dealing direct with the list owner, even if you can find him.

However, if you want to do your own research on available lists, numbers, rentals etc, the two books to consult are *Direct Marketing Services* and *BRAD Direct Marketing*.

You can, of course, always make direct approaches to any firm which you suspect might have a customer list of the profile you are looking for.

Security

List owners sometimes protect their lists by insisting that either they or an agreed mailing house should do the mailing for you, so that you never actually have the list in your possession. A more usual security system is to *seed* the list. This means that the owner scatters a few fictitious names (also known as *sleepers*) throughout the list at a variety of real addresses, possibly his own and those of friends, relatives, employees etc. In this way he is able to monitor any improper use of the list in future. The list owner can sue for breach of copyright if anyone uses his list without his permission.

Testing a list

With typical conversion rates of only 2 or 3 per cent – when you're succeeding – a test mailing of less than 1000 is unlikely to produce a statistically reliable result. So if you're using a list of less than 1000, just get on with it. Trying to sample the quality of a list this small isn't practicable.

Larger lists, however, should always be tested before committing yourself to a mass mailing. A list of 20,000 names, for example, will cost you £5000 or more to direct mail, so it makes sense to try just 1000 or so to estimate whether the larger mailing would be worth undertaking.

Unless this is your very first venture into direct mail, always test a new list by using a mailing piece which has produced satisfactory results with other lists. A test of this kind gives you two lots of information: the value of the new list in relation to other lists, and its absolute value for this particular mailing piece. By contrast, if you test a new list with a new mailing piece, you only get one answer to the double question *Does this mailshot work with this list?* And if the answer is *No*, you won't know whether to attribute the failure to the mailing piece or to the list, and so you'll be little wiser than when you started.

Most owners will allow you to test their lists on a small scale, and you should always take this opportunity if the numbers warrant it. To get a good sample for your test mailing, you may be offered *nth selections*, a sampling procedure which allows you to specify every 10th, 15th, 25th – or nth – name on the list. This spreads the samples throughout the list and so avoids your testing a possibly uncharacteristic concentration. A block of names from a list sorted geographically, for example, may leave you testing a thousand Glaswegians, who may or may not be typical of the list as a whole. So nth selections are a very good idea.

Putting the mailing piece together

Remember that a mailshot is an advertisement – a *single* advertisement. It may be composed of separate items, each to some degree an ad in its own right – the letter, sales literature, order form, reply envelope, etc – but the purpose of the whole is to convey a single coherent and favourable impression.

It's very easy to overlook the importance of the *packing* of the mailing piece – literally, the way the pieces are put together in the envelope.

Consider the wrapper – the outer envelope – first of all. This is the first thing the prospect sees. Does it look cheap and nasty? Or attractive and of good quality? Could it be seriously taken for an individually mailed business letter or does it unmistakably declare itself as a piece of advertising? Neither one is necessarily better than the other, but the style of the wrapper should match the style of the contents so that the mailing piece holds together from the start.

Choose a wrapper which can comfortably accommodate the contents. Any enclosure which has to be folded more than twice to make it fit is probably going to look a mess when it's unfolded. Further, the folds should not leave creases that break up the pattern of the artwork. Make sure that no fold with open-ended sides lies along the top edge of the envelope where it's at risk of being slit by a paper knife when the mailshot is first opened.

Don't fold enclosures into each other. The increased thickness will tend to make the folds messy, and the customer anyway has to separate the enclosures from each other to read them.

Keep the number of enclosures to a minimum, and ensure that the customer can easily see how they relate to each other. The more bits of paper you put into your package, the greater your risk of confusing the reader and losing him altogether. Make your letter *look* like a letter because that's the enclosure that the reader will naturally select first of all. Whatever else you say in the letter, use it to guide the reader to the other enclosures so that he knows what they're for and where he should go next.

Testing a mailshot

Any component of a mailshot may be tested by the *split mailing* technique. This is very like the A/B split runs in the press (see page 138). You prepare two versions of the mailshot, and send one version to one half of the people you mail, and the other version to the other half. A thousand names in each half should be adequate for the test. As with list testing above, you can secure a reliable sample by using nth names, but make sure that the A and B versions go out alternately to these names. If, for example, you're using every 10th name, send A to name 10, B to name 20, A to name 30, B to name 40, and so on. Don't make the mistake of sending version A to names 10, 20, 30 etc, and then version B to names 10,010, 10,020 etc, as the two halves of the list may not be homogeneous.

Above all, only test one variation at a time or your results will be useless. Suppose version B differs from version A in both sales letter and selling price, and suppose that you get no significant difference in response to the two versions. At first sight, it looks as if you've proved that A and B are just as good, or just as bad, as each other. But you *haven't* proved that; in fact you haven't proved anything. It is possible that the revised sales letter was less effective than the original one and actually lost you some customers at the same time as the reduced price attracted a similar number of extra customers who would not otherwise have made a purchase. Net result: no change. Had you tested each modification separately, you would have identified both the failure and the success, and by dropping the one and continuing with the other, you would have achieved a real improvement in your results.

Be a weight watcher

Don't wait until the sacks of mail are ready to be handed over to the Post Office before considering the weight of each item. While 1000 items weighing 60g each cost £180 for second-class postage, the same number of items at 61g each cost £280 (1992 rates). Watch the weights, and take them into account at each stage of your preparation. Don't for example, choose a paper for your sales literature merely on the basis of printing quality and 'feel'; you could land yourself with a needlessly high postal bill.

The lowest postage is for items of not more than 60g. The next lowest is for up to 100g, and then the tariff rises in 50g steps to 500g, in 100g steps to 700g, and a final 50g step to 750g – the maximum weight for the second-class letter post. Pick up a free leaflet giving full details at any post office.

Post Office facilities

The Royal Mail Response Services have already been mentioned (page 107). Other services of particular interest to the mail trader are listed below.

International Business Reply Service

This is similar to the inland Business Reply service. For international mail the annual licence fee is £300 (in 1992) entitling you to receive up to a thousand items per year without further charge; thereafter, each reply costs 30p.

Household Delivery Service

This is Royal Mail's unaddressed mail delivery service. Items are delivered along with the normal mail on a door-to-door basis. You can mail to any area, from one postcode sector upwards. No stamps are required and items can be enveloped or unenveloped. The Household Delivery Service is probably best used in conjunction with a geodemographic targeting system, as described earlier in the chapter.

Items weighing 60g – the maximum acceptable weight – cost £53 per thousand for a distribution size up to 20,000. Larger distributions and weights less than 35g per item attract lower charges. Apart from weight limits, there are also size limits, and items for the service have to be bundled in regular qualities – typically 100 per bundle – and delivered to the appropriate post office between a week and two weeks before the proposed distribution start date.

Admail

This is a redirection service, enabling you to receive mail at an address different from the one you use in your promotional material. It is intended to be used, for example, when you wish to advertise your head office address but have orders delivered direct to your response-handling agent. The Admail service is available, under contract, for fixed periods of between 30 and 365 days, at fees ranging from £100 to £600 (1992 rates).

Mailsort

Under this service you can obtain a discount on postage if you mail at least 4000 letters or 1000 packets at any one time. To qualify for the discount, you have to pre-sort the mailing according to Mailsort's sortation plan. This identifies 1520 of the Royal Mail's main Delivery Offices and the postcode areas served by each of these offices. It also identifies 84 Intermediate Sorting Offices to which mail is sent if there are not enough items for an individual Delivery Office. You pre-sort your mail in this way, bundling items together as appropriate, putting them in a bag and addressing the bag to the relevant Delivery Office or Intermediate Sorting Office. The bags are then collected by the Royal Mail and the rest of the delivery process is in their hands.

Discounts available under the Mailsort service depend upon the quantities mailed and the speed of delivery that you require. Discounts vary between 13 per cent and 32 per cent of the normal postage.

Chapter 11
Analysing the Results

At the heart of every advertising campaign there lies the question of cost. If you could place your advertising free of charge, send out mailshots free of charge, get in all the services and professional help you need free of charge, then it wouldn't matter if only one person in a million responded favourably. Any success, however small, would increase your wealth: no failure, however extensive, would diminish it.

Regrettably, the real world isn't like that. All your attempts to sell cost money, and each failure reduces your wealth just as each success adds to it.

Every campaign can finally be weighed in the balance. Put the cost of the failures in one scale, and the profit of the successes in the other, and the story is told. Notice that there are two ways of improving the balance: reduce the failures or increase the successes. The latter may look more dramatic but the former can be every bit as valuable.

Take an example. If you direct mail 1000 people at a cost of £350, each mailshot costs you 35p. If you succeed in making 20 sales at a gross profit of £20 each, then your advertising profit works out at (£20 × 20) – £350 = £50. If you could make one more sale, your profit would go up from £50 to £70 – a 40 per cent improvement. Not bad. But notice that virtually the same improvement would be made if you could identify in advance just 57 of the original 980 non-buyers, and so save the £20 you would otherwise have spent (ie 57 × 35p) uselessly mailing your advertising to them. You'll remember from the last chapter than 12 per cent of the names on a one-year-old list could well be useless – that's 120 per 1000. So the scope for improvement via the elimination of failures is considerable.

Note particularly that absolute numbers are without any significance at all. It does not matter how many hundreds of replies a particular ad attracts nor how many thousands of pounds' worth of sales it produces: what matters is that you should have more money at the end than you had at the beginning.

Don't rush to do things on the grand scale. The first task is to get the arithmetic to come out right, and you can normally work on that problem on a relatively small scale. Only when you are confident that you have solved that problem should you turn your attention to scaling up the size of the operation. Don't attempt to scale up an unprofitable campaign in the hope that something fundamental will happen to the underlying arithmetic. It won't. You will just turn small losses into large ones.

Working at a campaign is a matter of trying to calculate how best to spend your money so as to minimise your chance of failure and maximise your chance of success. The way to go about it is to record your results, analyse them, and see if the analysis points to areas of possible improvement.

Keeping the records

Once your business is of any size, you will almost certainly want to keep your records on a computer so that, with a suitable program, instant up-to-date analyses are available whenever you want them. But for the moment we are assuming that you keep your records manually. If nothing else, this has the merit of forcing you to understand the significance of the figures and the way the calculations need to be done.

Possible formats for an *Advertising Record Card* and *Advertising Results Summary* are shown on pages 156 and 159. These have already been completed with specimen details which are used later to illustrate the calculations. The formats are not to be regarded as the last word in form design, but the headings do show the kind of information you will probably want to include in your own record-keeping system.

The headings are commented on below. The marginal numbers match the superscript numbers on the forms, which have been included solely for the convenience of cross-reference; they are not integral parts of the record.

Advertising Record Card

1. *One-stage/two-stage.* Are you attempting to pull in immediate sales, or are you first inviting enquiries?
2. *Press/direct mail.* Is your initial or sole advertising in the press or the post?
3. *Publication.* If in the press, which paper?
4. *List.* If direct mailing, how many names and which list?
5. *Product.* Enough detail to enable you to distinguish the product from any others you also deal in.
6. *Date.* When was the ad published, or the mailing despatched?
7. *Description.* Any relevant details of the advertising not included elsewhere.
8. *Key.* The reference code of the advertisement.

ADVERTISING RECORD CARD

PROMOTION	Date[6] 29-7-92 Key[8] BW/6
One-stage/two-stage[1] TWO Press/direct mail[2] PRESS Publication[3] BARGAIN WEEKLY List[4] ⟋ Product[5] FAN (Model C)	Description[7] 7 SCC on household page P+P separately identified = £2
UNIT VALUES Product cost price[9] £ 9-00 " " selling price[10] £ 24-99 " " gross profit[11] £ 15-99	Advertising cost[12] £ 91-00 Mailshot cost[13] £ ⟋ Reply cost[14] £ 0-25 Despatch cost[15] £ 2-00
ANALYSIS DATE[16] 17-8-92 Enquiry cost[17] £ 1-69 Order cost[18] £ 14-97 Conversion[19] 12·96 %	 Total income[20] £ 188-93 LESS total outlay[21] £ 181-50 Profit/Loss[22] £ 7-43

9. *Product cost price.* The unit price you have to pay for the product you're selling.
10. *Product selling price.* The unit price you charge your customers.
11. *Product gross profit.* The difference between 9 and 10 above.
12. *Advertising cost.* The cost of the ad in the press or of the direct mailing.
13. *Mailshot cost.* If direct mailing, the cost per item.
14. *Reply cost.* This is the cost to you of a reply, in the post, sent in response to an enquiry prompted by stage one of a two-stage selling operation. It is the total cost of postage, enclosures, envelope, and – possibly – labour of a single reply.

   Note that reply cost is calculated on the assumption that all prepared and printed material will be used. If this turns out not to be so, your actual reply cost will have been higher. For example, suppose you had 500 sales letters printed for £15; that means that the sales letter component of your reply cost is £15 ÷ 500 = 3p. But if in the event you only used 250 of the letters, the remainder are now just worthless scrap, and the effective cost, therefore, of those you have used doubles to 6p each.

The purpose, however, of working out reply cost and all the other calculations is to help you decide upon future tactics, and for this the above assumption must be made, otherwise the figures would be distorted by the expectation of failure.

15. *Despatch cost.* This is the actual p&p cost to you of mailing a single order to a customer.

16. *Analysis date.* The remaining figures on the Advertising Record Card are calculated in part from the totals taken from the Advertising Results Summary. Until the last result is in – and you will never know that it *is* because tomorrow may always bring just one more – the analysis is true only at the date when you make the calculation. Put the date here, so that you can later know up to and including which results the analysis is based upon.

17. *Enquiry cost.* You have an enquiry cost in two-stage selling only. It is the amount you turn out to have spent on advertising in order to get in one enquiry. This is the formula:

Advertising cost ÷ No of enquiries

If your advertising cost is £91 and you pull in 54 enquiries, then your enquiry cost is £91 ÷ 54 = £1.69.

18. *Order cost.* This is the amount you turn out to have spent in order to pull in a single order. This is the formula:

(Enquiry cost + Reply cost) × (No of enquiries ÷ No of sales)

If enquiry cost is £1.69, reply cost 25p, and you get 54 enquiries and 7 sales, then your order cost is (£1.69 + 25p) × (54 ÷ 7) = £14.97.

19. *Conversion.* This is the number of sales you make, expressed as a percentage of the number of mailshots, whether as replies to enquirers in two-stage selling or as the total number of items in a one-stage direct mailing. This is the formula:

(No of sales ÷ No of mailshots) × 100

If you make 7 sales as the result of sending 54 replies to enquirers, your conversion is (7 ÷ 54) × 100 = 12.96 per cent.

The conversion figure is particularly useful when you wish to compare the results of different campaigns.

20. *Total income.* This is the total amount of money your customers send you as a result of this particular promotion. Take the figure from the totals line of the income column on the Advertising Results Summary – £188.93 on the specimen form.

21. *Total outlay.* This is the formula:

Advertising cost + (Reply cost × No of enquiries)
+ Fulfilment cost

Take the fulfilment figure from the totals line of the fulfilment column on the Advertising Results Summary. If advertising cost is £91, reply cost 25p, number of enquiries 54 and fulfilment cost £77, then your total outlay is £91 + (25p × 54) + £77 = £181.50.

22. *Profit or loss.* This, of course, is the most important figure of all. The formula is:

Total income – Total outlay

If total income is £188.93 and total outlay is £181.50, then your result is £188.93 – £181.50 = £7.43: you have made a profit of £7.43.

Advertising Results Summary

23. *Date.* The particular day whose results you are recording.
24. *Enquiries.* The number of enquiries that day.
25. *Sales.* The number of sales that day.
26. *Returns.* The number of items returned for refund that day.
27. *Income.* The total amount of money received that day from customers responding to the advertised offer (both for the product and p&p) minus the value of any refunds made for returned goods.
28. *Fulfilment.* The total cost to you of fulfilling the day's orders. If you're selling a single product, the formula is:

(Product cost price + Despatch cost) × No of sales

If you're offering a choice of products, you will have to work out the figure by totalling actual fulfilment costs of each sale, ie the cost to you of the products sold that day plus the cost of packing and mailing them.
29. *Comments.* Use this space to note anything that throws light on the day's results.

Chuck it, change it or raise the stakes?

The purpose of the record and the analysis is to help you decide whether to ditch the campaign altogether, modify it in the hope of improving the results, or keep it as it is but scaled up so that you can start making some respectable profits.

ADVERTISING RESULTS SUMMARY

Key **BW/6**

Date[23]	Enqs[24]	Sales[25]	Returns[26]	Income[27]		Fulfilment[28]		Comments[29]
July 30	0							
31	2							
Aug. 1	3							
2	—							No Post — local strike
4	12							
5	9	2		53	98	22	00	
6	9	2		53	98	22	00	
7	5							
8	3							
9	3	1		26	99	11	00	
11	2							
12	5	1		26	99	11	00	
13	—							Office closed for the day.
14	0	1		26	99	11	00	
15	1							
16	0							
TOTALS	54	7		188	93	77	00	

The first figure to consider is the last one on your Advertising Record Card: profit/loss.

If you've made a large loss

It is not worth trying to improve an advertising operation whose results have been nowhere near success. Improvements are always of a marginal nature and are therefore worth going for only when the problem itself is marginal. If at first you are selling two items a week and you calculate that to make a profit you need to sell a further 39 items a week, then forget it. You are so far from the required figure that it is clear that your operation is fundamentally unsound and no amount of tinkering with this element or that is going to be of any use. Scrap the whole thing and start again.

Regard a loss as large if even a 25 per cent increase in your sales figures would still leave you losing money.

If you've made a small loss or a small profit

With a marginal loss or a marginal profit, you should look closely at your results to see if there is anywhere you might effect improvements. Consider every figure in turn.

A worked example

The following comments, using the figures on the specimen forms, illustrate how you might mull over your problem.

What's my position? The profit/loss figure[22] shows I made a profit of £7.43. Well, at least the balance is in my favour. It would, however, have needed only one customer to change his mind on the way to the post, and instead of a small profit I would have made a small loss. I clearly need to get the campaign more soundly based before attempting to scale things up. Where could I get an improvement?

Product cost price.[9] The product costs me £9. Could I purchase more cheaply? Could I get a greater discount by buying larger quantities? Could I buy more cheaply from another source? From another wholesaler? Direct from the manufacturer? Could I find a similar product more cheaply priced? Could I make a similar product myself, or have it made to my specification, at a lower price?

I doubt if I could shave more than 50p or so off my cost – worth trying for, but not by itself very significant.

Product selling price.[10] I'm selling for £24.99. Could I sell for more? If I were to sell for, say, £29.99 without reducing my number of sales, that would give me another £35 and make my profit much more healthy at something over £40. On the other hand, if the higher price lost me only a single sale, I'd be very little better off than I am now. And anyway, at the higher price, the product would be looking decidedly expensive. So that doesn't look too hopeful. Perhaps I could get away with a smaller price increase – £2 perhaps. I might try it.

Advertising cost.[12] The ad costs me £91 for 7 scc. That's an scc rate of £13.

Most of the other advertisers on the page use 5 scc spaces. If I could cut my ad down to that size, I would save £26. Worth considering, especially in conjunction with some other marginal changes.

Reply cost.[14] At only 25p, my total expenditure for the 54 replies only comes to £13.50, and with postage alone accounting for over half that, there's very little saving to be made here. Don't bother.

Despatch cost.[15] The product, packed for despatch, weighs 750g, and so can just be mailed as a package in the second-class post at £1.40 (1992 rates). Packaging is costing me 60p a time, so it looks as if I might be able to make a small saving here. If, for example, I could halve the packaging costs, I would make an extra 30p per order, and on the seven sales achieved, my profit would rise from £7.43 to £9.53. Certainly worth looking at.

Enquiry cost.[17] The ad pulls in 54 enquiries at £1.69 each. Of course, if I reduced the size of the ad without reducing the number of enquiries, enquiry cost would automatically improve anyway. But the question is: could I get in *more* useful enquiries? Since I can only sell to people who enquire in the first place, the number of enquiries sets a limit on my sales potential. What if I used a Freepost address? Or a telephone number for people to ring in to ask for details to be sent to them? Worth considering.

Order cost.[18] The only component of the order cost that I've not so far considered is the number of sales. If instead of making seven sales, I could make 10 or 11 to the same number of enquirers, that would radically change the story. Perhaps I should include further inducements to purchase in my reply mailing. Such inducements would only increase my cost in proportion to the number of sales. Suppose I offered every purchaser a free gift, which in fact cost me, say, 50p? That would reduce my gross profit by 50p a customer, leaving me with an approximate gross £15.50 a time instead of £16 as now. But even a single extra customer would justify the expense because 8 × £15.50 = £124 whereas 7 × £16 = £112. Looks a good idea, if I could find a suitable gift.

What about a second reply mailing to the non-buyers after the first reply? Perhaps I need only offer the free gift in this second mailing? If a second reply cost the same as the first reply, even a single extra sale to the original 47 non-buyers would be to my advantage. Looks an even better idea.

Conversion.[19] The present conversion – virtually 13 per cent – looks fairly respectable, but in other two-stage campaigns I've got as high as 20 per cent with a similar product, so I feel it's worth nagging away at this one for a bit longer. Even 16 or 17 per cent would mean another couple of sales – definitely worth going for – so I don't think I'm being unrealistic.

Conclusion. The ad looks promising, but the margin of success is too small for comfort. I'll see if I can implement any of the above ideas, and test their effects on the results. Where appropriate I might use an A/B split run for the ad; unfortunately, the present numbers are far too small to justify a split mailing test of the reply to enquirers.

What sort of improvements yield the best results?
Part of every mail order operation is on public view – the ad, the sales letter, the selling price, and so on. These are the things that are known to the public and that influence them in their decisions to enquire or not to enquire, to buy or not to buy.

Another part of the mail order operation is concealed from the public – your product cost price, your postage costs, stationery costs, and so on – and therefore has no effect on their decisions. It follows from this that any improvement made to the concealed part of a mail order operation is virtually certain to be reflected in improved results, whereas an attempt to improve the public part of the operation is always speculative. If at all possible, go for concealed improvements.

How many returns can you expect?

In the worked example above, we had no returns, not a very common situation. But while returns complicate the calculations, they don't fundamentally change them, and so we did without returns for the purpose of the example.

In reality, in any campaign of any size, you can expect returns for refund: perhaps 1 per cent, perhaps 5 per cent, perhaps 10 per cent. There's no general rule. What matters is that any returns at all increase your costs in the form of extra postage, packing etc, and furthermore, not all returned goods will arrive back with you in a resaleable condition, and that can be the heaviest extra cost of all.

But as with everything in the business, it's all a matter of expenditure and income, and the degree to which at the end of the day the latter exceeds the former. The objective is not to minimise the number of returns, but to maximise the ultimate profits. It may be far better to take orders from 100 customers, 10 per cent of whom later require refunds, than to take orders from 50 customers, none of whom requires a refund.

Look at it like this. When people read your advertising, they do not immediately polarise into two groups, one of which is totally committed to taking up your offer and the other of which totally rejects it. Certainly there may be some people at one or other of these extremes, but most people will lie between them, shading down from all but total commitment to all but total rejection.

The most crucial part of this spectrum from your point of view is the middle section: these are the people who read your advertising with interest, are tempted by your offer, but come to no quick or clear decision to act on it. The people at the extremes are either yours already or will never be yours; those susceptible to persuasion must be in the middle section. A marginally lower price, a more detailed description, a more urgent style of wording, a more attractive illustration – these are the sorts of things that might persuade the ditherers to place an order.

But people who are susceptible to persuasion in one direction are just as susceptible to it in another, and it is reasonable to expect a higher proportion of returns from those people who only marginally felt themselves persuaded into making a purchase. Provided you're making a comfortable profit, however, these returns shouldn't worry you.

Paradoxically, you may have a cause for worry if you're getting *too few* returns. However marvellous your product, you cannot hope to please all of the people all of the time. If you're getting a very low level of returns, it may be because you are succeeding in selling only to those people at one extreme of the spectrum: the totally committed. Perhaps all those ditherers in the middle section, having had their interest aroused by your advertising, think about your offer but can find nothing further in it to tempt them into making a purchase. Too few returns may be a warning signal to you that your sales message isn't powerful enough; you could be losing customers needing only a slight push to get them to make a purchase.

Will results improve with successive insertions of an advertisement?

It has been said elsewhere that no press add should be judged on the result of a single insertion. Run it three or four times unchanged to average out freak fluctuations.

That being said, the general tendency is for results to decline, although a really successful ad might hold steady for a long period, possibly for years. Even when a paper's circulation figures are stable, there is a continuous coming and going of readers: old readers drop out, new ones take their place. The steady success of any given ad is probably attributable to this turnover in readership. Suppose, for example, that 10 per cent of last week's readers drop out and a new 10 per cent take their place. If you advertised for the first time last week, your ad was new to 100 per cent of the readership; this week it's new to only 10 per cent. This explains why results tend to decline: in successive issues of the same paper, you are largely talking to the same people. If they were not interested in your product at first, they are unlikely to acquire an interest by seeing the same ad week after week.

There is a slight counterpressure to this decline. Someone who all but decided to respond to your ad last week may be pushed over the threshold into action by seeing it again this week. The net effect, however, of a series of ads over an extended period is usually one of decline.

If your experimental advertising shows a large profit

Don't worry about long-term declines if your current advertising shows a healthy profit. If that happens, you've every reason to feel pleased. You've got the arithmetic right, and you have the makings of a successful campaign. Now is the time to start thinking about scaling up the size of the operation. You're on your way.

Appendices

Some Products Considered

The list that follows has two purposes: to stir up your ideas if you're still looking for something to sell by mail, and to show by example the typical first weighing-up of the pros and cons of a product – using the criteria set out in Chapter 3 – which the intending trader must undertake. Note that the term *product* includes both goods and services.

The list is not, of course, a list of recommended products – that's just not possible. *Your* product must suit your own knowledge, skills and circumstances; no one else can make choices for you. Use the list as a prompt, not as a crib.

Ancestor tracing
This differs from most mail order businesses in one important respect: that most of the work is done outside the business premises and involves travelling to many different places to undertake the research needed to sustain the service.

The major cost of the service arises from the individual research the business requires. This is very demanding of time and expertise, and offers little chance to make savings through economies of scale that help to bring down costs in most businesses as they grow. But most of the other mail order features are very favourable: handling, mailing etc present no difficulties. Product price may need to be tailored to individual clients and their special problems, and should be realistically pitched to cover all your expenses. A time-consuming service of this kind cannot be cheap.

Advertise up-market. You need clients with money, and money acquired relatively recently. Those with inherited wealth are likely to know all about their ancestors anyway. Try advertising in the papers read by professional and successful business people. Mail order, never less than nationwide, could in this case be worldwide. Foreign nationals seeking British ancestry could be very promising clients; the American market particularly should be worth getting into.

Follow-up possibilities are pretty thin. The best that you can hope for is that satisfied clients will recommend you to their friends.

Audio equipment

The mail order appeal of audio equipment is as for many other items which need to be *used* by the customer before he knows it has the qualities he really wants. Buying any sort of audio equipment in a high street shop is always a lottery: it's easy to judge which machines look good and have the range of features one seeks, but judging the crucial quality of sound is virtually impossible in the noisy, bustling environment of a shop. The essence of the mail order appeal is *Try it in the quiet of your home; return it if dissatisfied.*

There is an enormous range of audio equipment on the market, some of it very compact and lightweight and therefore easy to handle and mail, with a good price/weight ratio. Personal stereos are worth considering as particularly convenient to deal with, but larger and heavier equipment need not be ruled out as it is usually well packed by manufacturers and should not suffer in transit unless deliberately mishandled.

Follow-up possibilities include records for record players; cassettes, blank and pre-recorded, for cassette players; and accessories – head-phones, extension speakers etc – for everything.

Bags and cases

Holdalls, handbags, briefcases, shoulder bags, suitcases etc are widely available in the shops, so the mail trader must look for some special selling feature in the items he plans to promote. Concentrate on a single item or set of items in your advertising which, ideally, should be illustrated. Look for items with a large number of useful features to which your advertising can draw attention, such things as special pockets for credit cards, passport, cheque book; well-concealed and zipped pockets for cash; cases that can open out at need to form larger cases; cases that can fold down to pocket size when not in use; and so on.

Though some of the large cases are bulky, none is difficult to mail or needs very much packing for secure transit. Sets of cases can often be packed one inside another, thus simplifying despatch.

You can lift your advertising pitch out of the rut by offering to have the owner's initials embossed on the product. Set up an arrangement with a local firm to do this work for you quickly and at no great cost, and allow for that cost in your all-in price to the customer so that you can offer personalised luggage for no more than the price of the luggage itself.

While most people have only a limited need for large travelling cases, smaller items like handbags, for example, have a strong fashion element to them, and follow-up sales of other designs should be possible.

Bedding

Plain sheets, fitted sheets, pillow cases, blankets, Continental quilts, eiderdowns – every household has a number of sets of bedding, and though these items are not bought frequently by any given household, the number of households in the market at any one time is very large and spread over the entire population.

Though some of the items are bulky, all are easy to handle and to pack, and short of direct vandalism are virtually damage-proof in transit. Provided you deal only in products of good quality, after-sales problems should be minimal.

The price/weight ratio is acceptable and the prices of the items high enough to justify the cost of a well-mounted advertising campaign. While all items can be sold singly, complete matching sets make attractive mail order offers either as gifts – to newly-weds and others setting up home for the first time – or as necessary items for the buyer's own use.

Follow-up items include other household textiles and fabrics, and indeed all other items of general household interest.

Bicycles

The bicycle as a means of cheap and healthy transport has greatly increased in popularity in recent years. Even so, specialist bicycle shops are not numerous, and mail order is worth considering as a retailing method, particularly for bicycles which are a little out of the ordinary. Consider folding bicycles, for example. These have all the characteristics of bikes in general, but they also have a certain gadgety appeal, a recurrent theme in mail order. They fold down for easy storage at home or in the boot of a car or even into a bag which may be easily carried. The owner can, for example, ride his bike to the station in the morning, fold it into the bag, take the train to town, and then cycle to the office at the other end, hanging his bike up in the cloakroom until he needs it again to go home. Features like these provide excellent material for the advertising copywriter.

From the customer's point of view, there is the further mail order appeal of the chance to try the machine out for a few days, secure in the knowledge that it can be returned for refund within the trial period. This is particularly important as many potential purchasers will be doubtful whether they have the skill, strength and stamina to use the bicycle to advantage.

If your product is a good one, after-sales problems should be minimal though some are bound to occur and you must be sure in advance that you have the organisation and skills to deal with them. Handling and mailing are obviously more awkward than with many products; you

169

need warehouse space and will probably have to use a non-Post Office carrier. Price/weight ratio is good.

There are no immediately obvious follow-ups; much depends upon the nature of your original sales pitch and the places you advertise. If you sell through cycling journals – and therefore to enthusiasts – you could follow up with other products of the outdoor life, such as camping gear. If you sell through general papers, promoting your product as a means of economical commuter transport, you might follow up with other items which promise to cut the cost of living, such things as devices to reduce home heating bills, or items of self-sufficiency appeal for growing your own food or brewing your own beer.

Binoculars/telescopes
There is a very wide range of such optical equipment available. At the top end of the range, items retail at £100 or more, and clearly this is not a good product for the non-specialist mail order beginner to choose. But at the bottom end of the market, the near-toys need not cost very much at all, and have a strong appeal to the buyer.

Binoculars confer *power*. You can see things other people can't see. And at a more mature level, you can use them in sport, for bird-watching, satellite spotting, and so on.

Cheap binoculars may be lightweight, and even good quality glasses with, say a 10 × 50 lens, may not weigh more than a kilogram. The glasses may come in boxes with good manufacturers' packing, needing only a little more outer wrapping for mailing. Price/weight ratio is very favourable for expensive glasses; indeed, there are many superb glasses specifically made to a very light weight, but that could take you into the £200-plus class where even with postal insurance the mailing costs are relatively insignificant.

Theatre glasses may be worth considering. These are always light in weight, and can make an attractive offer in the gift market.

Even cheap binoculars and telescopes should have a very long working life, and any optical products worthy of the name should give rise to few after-sales problems.

Books
Many people live within reach of a bookshop, and most people live within reach of a shop selling books, but shops of both kinds necessarily cater for the general interest. It is very difficult for the mail order bookseller to compete with the shops for the sale of the most popular titles; the Net Book Agreement ensures that most books are sold at fixed prices determined by the publishers, and so have to be sold for the same price whether the seller is a high street city bookshop or a one-man mail

trader operating out of his garden shed. Furthermore, the discount publishers usually allow to booksellers is too small to support a mail order operation, being about a third of the retail price rather than the two-thirds that the mail trader typically needs.

However, mail order is worth thinking about for books of special interest, ie ones that are not normally found on the shelves of the high street shops, provided that you can get your advertising to the specialist market and there is a sufficient number of buyers in the market and a sufficient number of titles that you can offer them.

Buying and selling secondhand books within a specialist area is also a mail order possibility, as is the trade in remainders (ie publishers' unwanted stock sold off to the trade at low prices and not subject to any kind of resale price maintenance).

Books are easy to pack, easy to mail, and with no working parts to go wrong. Follow-up possibilities are good: more of the same. Keep your customers posted with your latest catalogues.

Most mail ordering bookselling is in fact undertaken by publishers direct selling their own titles. To enter the market by this route, you need to have a good number of titles, and the confidence – and money – to have them printed ready to sell by mail before you have any evidence whether they will sell at all. One possible approach is to start by selling books of similar interest published by other people; then once you are sure that the market exists and you can reach it, you can start publishing your own titles, and one by one substitute your own books for those of other publishers on your list.

Calculators

An enormous variety of calculators is available, some little bigger than credit cards, others large enough to be convenient for desktop work, some that also tell the time, play tunes, print calculations, and so on. At the top end of the market are the programmable calculators, which might fairly be regarded as the bottom end of the computer market, but at the more humble level there are low-priced calculators offering a range of functions to meet most needs, mathematical, scientific, financial, or just plain old-fashioned adding, subtracting, multiplying and dividing.

Most calculators are small, lightweight and easy to mail. The price/weight ratio is favourable. Though calculators *can* go wrong after sale, most are well made and reliable, and the virtual absence of mechanical parts, except in the printing models, means in practice that most calculators live out a useful life without anything ever going wrong.

Although calculators are widely available, most are sold in a take-it-or-leave-it fashion by shops whose assistants frequently understand little

171

of the capabilities and applications of the products they sell. This is where the mail trader can score. Produce sales literature that lovingly specifies every last thing that the calculator can do, and the way it does it. Give worked examples of different calculations, showing how the problems would be keyed into the machine and how the answers would be displayed.

Use either display advertising for off-the-page selling or classified advertising for two-stage selling.

There are many opportunities for follow-up sales to satisfied customers: more complicated calculators, other microchip-based devices – electronic games, home computers, clocks, watches, and so on. You can also follow up with items of related interest; for example, someone buying a calculator with a number of specifically business-type functions could well be amenable to offers of other business equipment, such as typewriters, telephones, photocopiers.

Camping equipment

Tents, groundsheets etc have a good price/weight ratio, are fairly easy to handle and despatch, and are unlikely to give rise to many after-sales problems. Illustrated advertising is best but classified two-stage advertising should also be considered.

Follow-up possibilities include backpacks, hiking boots, compasses and all the other items appealing to those who like the outdoor life. The trade tends to be seasonal, but the real enthusiasts are in the market for equipment long before the time they hope to use it. Advertise in the specialist magazines catering for hikers, campers, ramblers, cyclists, motor cyclists etc.

Car accessories

There is a huge range of accessories available for enthusiastic car owners, and once you have attracted customers and satisfied them with your service, you should be able to look forward to a regular flow of orders, though you will, of course, need to stock a suitable selection of items and keep your catalogue attractive and up-to-date. Some of the many possible opening offers are considered below.

Car burglar alarms

Next to his house, his car is often the most expensive of a person's possessions. The cost and difficulty of fitting an anti-thief device are trivial compared with the cost and inconvenience of having one's car stolen. Car burglar alarms can be small, light and easy to mail, and, if properly installed by the purchaser, should not give rise to excessive claims for repair or replacement.

Car compasses

These are popular with keen motorists, particularly those compasses that fix to the dashboard. There are also the novelty kind that attach to a car key ring. Both kinds are easy to mail, the latter particularly so.

Car ramps

For the man who likes servicing his own car, a pair of ramps that allow him to work comfortably underneath it are a great advantage. Fairly small, easily mailed, and with no working parts to go wrong, they are well suited to mail order selling, and may be promoted as a pleasing gift for the motorist on, for example, the run-up to Christmas. They will, of course, appeal to the motorist himself all the year round.

Car vacuum cleaners

Mini vacuum cleaners that can easily get into the crevices in the limited space of a car interior make popular mail order lines. They can, of course, also be used for other purposes, such as cleaning up armchairs and other upholstered furniture. They are light and easy to use, and light and easy to mail. Naturally, they have working parts and are therefore subject to mechanical and electrical failure.

Cassettes: audio and video

Though readily available in the high street shops, these are well worth considering for mail order because of the repeat orders which should come from satisfied customers. If you can attract a sufficient number of regular customers, your business will develop a momentum of its own.

Cassettes are very easy to mail, and the well-known brands should cause few after-sales problems. Blanks are obviously easier to deal in than pre-recorded tapes, but the latter are worth considering even though you will require a much more varied and therefore more risky stock. However, having contacted people with audio and video equipment, the offer of pre-recorded material is an obvious follow-up and one you may like to try.

Children's wear

The mail order appeal of children's wear is almost always one of price. Have a catalogue of the items you offer for sale, illustrated where possible, giving full details of sizes, colours available, etc. Advertise your catalogue either free, or at nominal cost to cover your expenses, or for an SAE. Classified advertising should be satisfactory, using such a headline as *QUALITY CHILDREN'S CLOTHES AT BARGAIN PRICES.*

The price/weight ratio is favourable, and the clothes are easy to handle, easy to pack, not susceptible to damage in the post, and ought not to give rise to problems after sale. Since children are always growing, the follow-up possibilities of further clothing are obvious. The satisfied customer, however, may also be interested in clothes for herself and other adult members of the family – but, again, the appeal should be one of quality at low prices.

Bear in mind that the satisfied customer will be familiar with the quality of your products, so that the mail trader's difficulty in conveying a sense of the quality of his product has largely vanished by the time of the second purchase.

Other follow-ups, particularly towards Christmas, include children's games, toys, books, and so on. And don't forget that the start of the school year is a time when special sportswear and school clothing are required.

Coins and medals

Small, easily handled, easily mailed, coins and medals make very convenient mail order items. They are also very easily described as they need only be named for collectors to know exactly which coin or medal is in question; and although quality is less simply characterised, it is very much easier to define than for most products because of the standard phrases used by dealers and collectors which identify an item's quality within fairly narrow limits. As a result, coins and medals can be sold by classified advertising and from unillustrated catalogues.

Dealing in coins and medals is, of course, a matter of both buying and selling. Unlike retailing, where goods pass from manufacturer to wholesaler to mail order dealer to the public, the coin and medal business is a ping-pong game between dealer and public, goods moving from the public to the dealer and then back again from the dealer to the public. Sometimes dealers trade among themselves, and sometimes indeed the public do, and there are auctions at which all the combinations of dealer to dealer, dealer to public, public to dealer, and public to public may be found. In the main, however, the coin and medal business is from public to dealer and back again, and the mail order dealer must be able to get his prices right when both buying and selling.

Unlike the retailer of normal consumer products, the dealer can't establish what the trade price is and then work out his own selling price accordingly, confident that he can always pick up further supplies at a known price if he gets a sudden rush of orders. If the coin and medal dealer gets a sudden rush of orders for a given item, he is likely to find himself having to buy in extra stock at a premium. The dealer has to perform a delicate balancing act if he is to pitch his selling prices attractively and yet cover his costs and show a profit. The balancing act is made the more difficult by the inevitable delays between placing advertising and having it published, and between drafting pricelists and having them printed. And yet if you are knowledgeable and able to deal shrewdly, coin and medal dealing can make a profitable mail order business.

Computer software

The micro computer is moving – though perhaps not quite as fast as seemed likely a few years ago – towards the time when it will be as commonplace in the average home as the record player or cassette recorder. Although the enthusiasts will continue to be fascinated with computers *as* computers – just as there are hi-fi buffs more concerned with frequency response than with music – most people in the end will want their computers to *do* something, either useful or entertaining, and the demand for computer software – the programs that are to computers what records are to record players – can do nothing but grow.

Programs may be on tape, disc, cartridge or ROM, or the very simplest may be no more than a printed listing for the user to copy on to his own machine. All of them are very easy to mail with little to go wrong unless they are negligently handled.

You could market the programs that other people have created, or you could write your own if you have the very special flair that this requires.

Advertise, at first, in the computer journals. In time, however, when the computer has become a routine piece of domestic equipment, you will probably want to advertise in places appropriate to the subject matter of the particular programs you deal in.

Computers

Small, relatively cheap computers are easy to pack and mail. As the domestic television set is normally pressed into service as the VDU, the need to mail this most fragile part of the system is avoided.

The cheapest computers are increasingly being sold in high street shops, along with TV, radio and hi-fi equipment, but the amount of informed assistance that staff in such shops are able to give to customers is typically rather low. So much the better for the mail order trade.

Let your advertising and sales literature give full technical details of the product, though if you are aiming at the first-time buyer, make sure the information is couched in language that an intelligent layman can understand. Technicalities are unavoidable, but there is no reason why plain English explanations of those technicalities should not be given so that the inexperienced purchaser can feel confident that he knows what he is buying. Follow-ups include computer software (see above) and computer peripherals: printers, program storage devices, etc.

Correspondence courses

There is no market in retailing other publishers' correspondence courses, but if you are able to write a course yourself on a subject in which you are suitably qualified, teaching by correspondence can make a very good mail order business. The business has two elements to it: the provision of course material, and the marking and supervision of students' work. Whatever the subject matter, the course material and the student supervision both need to be of a high standard – certainly not less than the standard you would expect of a specialist full-time schoolteacher or a college lecturer in the subject.

Correspondence courses are in their nature specially designed to exploit the postal service and so, not surprisingly, they have many favourable mail order characteristics. Almost exclusively, they are composed of written or printed material which is ideal for mailing, easily handled, difficult to damage in transit, with a good price/weight ratio.

Among the difficulties are that the market is well served by long-established schools offering a range of all the more popular subjects. A costly, sustained and highly professional advertising campaign would be needed to win a share of the popular market; but if you are offering only one subject, such a campaign is clearly out of the question. Perhaps a beginner hoping to make an effective entrance into the market should be one who can promote himself as a skilled practitioner in the field offered as a course of study, for example *WRITE FOR TV. Successful TV playwright offers personal postal tuition to new writers.*

Even a single subject, provided you get enough students, can make at least a part-time venture, though like any business based upon the sale of your skilled personal attention, its scope for expansion is limited by the amount of work you can reasonably fit into the available time. Virtually limitless expansion, however, is possible by commissioning other experts to write – and supervise – courses on other subjects which can then be offered through your school.

Craft supplies

There is a large range of possibilities under this heading. The enthusiasts of this craft or that – knitting, jewellery making, pottery, leatherwork, marquetry, painting, toy making, modelling etc – have a continuing need for the raw materials of their crafts, appropriate craft tools and books on the subject. Few people live within easy reach of a shop that can cater for the needs of their particular craft, and it is this that gives such products their mail order appeal.

Advertise in the relevant hobby journals. With many crafts, you may be able to start your business with no more in the way of advertising than a simple printed list of items and prices sent to enquirers responding to your classified advertising.

Most raw materials are easy to pack and mail and have a good price/weight ratio. Satisfied customers can be expected to re-order basic supplies regularly, and they will also be in the market for occasional purchases of equipment.

Curtains

Various mail order opportunities can be considered here. If you are a skilled curtain maker you could offer a made-to-measure service, sending sets of specimen materials to prospective customers, together with instructions on how to measure up windows. Such a service could be advertised in the personal columns of papers and magazines.

Alternatively, you could deal in ready-made curtains of standard lengths; these are probably best sold from full-colour display advertising. Or you could deal simply in curtaining materials, selling lengths for customers to make up themselves.

Easy to pack and mail, with virtually no risk of transit damage, curtains are unlikely to cause after-sales problems as little can go wrong beyond stitching coming adrift, and that should certainly not happen in any properly made curtains.

Because heavy drapes tend to be more expensive than lightweight ones, a good price/weight ratio should be maintained throughout the range. Follow-up possibilities are, first and foremost, more curtains; every home has many windows, and customers who have used your service for one room are obvious targets for follow-up sales for their other rooms.

Don't forget net curtains as well – even easier to handle and mail than drapes.

Developing and printing service

Although this is the sort of service offered by large photographic processing laboratories, there is no reason why the small mail order service should not set up in this field. If you use pre-printed envelopes with a Freepost address, it is very easy for your customers to mail you their films, and the finished negatives/slides/prints are easily mailed back. You must, of course, be a competent processor and have suitable equipment, but provided these two conditions are met, you should have few after-sales problems. The real problems are before-sales ones: getting the customers. The competition is cut-throat, the major laboratories offering such inducements as free films and 24-hour processing.

Try advertising for customers with simple classified advertising at holiday times in popular papers, inviting people either to send their films to you or to ask for details of your service. It would help if you could persuade shops, hotels and restaurants in suitable locations to hold supplies of your reply envelopes for the convenience of their customers. Alternatively, yours could be a mail order service for these other traders, who would mail their customers' films to you in bulk.

Follow-up possibilities include the sale of photo display goods – albums, frames etc – and further prints and selective enlargements of customers' favourite pictures, perhaps made up as greeting cards, or wall calendars or posters. But the main follow-up is simply the repeat order: enclose a fresh reply envelope with every returned film, and satisfied customers will use your service again.

Electric drills

After a hammer and screwdriver, the electric drill is probably the DIY enthusiast's most used and most useful tool. With different accessories it is also a versatile tool, and the mail order selling of the drill itself plus a whole collection of accessories has been popular for a number of years. Though relatively heavy, packing is not difficult since the drills usually come in makers' cartons which may only need outer wrapping to make them suitable for transit through the mail.

The price/weight ratio, however, may be a problem. As with all mechanical things, there is bound to be a certain number of drills that will fail to operate satisfactorily or even break down altogether. It is at this point, rather than at the time of sale, that the weight of the drill becomes a nuisance. Unless a very simple repair is all that is needed – and it is also within your competence – you will have to return the drill to the manufacturer for repair, and although the repair during the guarantee period may be free, you will have to bear the cost of getting the drill to the manufacturer, and then have the cost of returning the repaired drill to your customer. You may also wish to reimburse the customer's costs in returning the drill to you in the first place.

It may be that the customer chooses to deal direct with the manufacturer and that the manufacturer is prepared to deal direct with your customer; but remember that the customer's contract in law is with you as the retailer, and he is entirely within his rights to return unsatisfactory equipment to you and to insist that you deal with the problem. The cost to you of dealing with problems of this kind can take a substantial bite out of the profit you hoped to get from the original sale. For this reason if for no other, you should choose the equipment you sell with the greatest care, preferring the reliable to the cheap, because the cheap isn't cheap if you have excessive costs dealing with returned goods. But even the best drills will give rise to *some* returns, and you must allow for this in the price you charge.

Figurines

All sorts of figurines are popular as household ornaments. Some are made in distinctive styles so that different figurines form part of a series and therefore appeal as *collectibles*, and hence generate their own follow-up orders.

If you manufacture the figurines yourself, take account of possible mailing problems in your designs. For example, favour figurines of compact shape without fragile protuberances, such as a model of an angler with a thin extended rod. Items like this can be very difficult to pack and mail securely, and breakages may reach a level which renders the whole operation uneconomic. Of course, the material which the figurine is made of has an important bearing on the problem, and you would not want to embark on the manufacture of items, however charming, which in their very nature are unlikely to withstand the rigours of mailing very well.

Specially formed expanded polystyrene packs make excellent damage-proof mailing boxes, but the more specialised your packaging, the less flexible your mail order operation. Try not to be too committed to a particular item in a particular pack before having the experience to judge whether this is precisely what the market requires.

If you do not manufacture the product yourself, consider seeking out less well-known manufacturers, either at home or abroad, so that your items have a freshness of appeal.

Advertising obviously needs to be well illustrated. The cost of mounting a mail order operation in items of this kind is quite high, so be sure to choose figurines which you can reasonably expect to command a sufficiently high price.

Fire and burglar alarms

Devices to give warning of fire or break-in vary considerably both in their degree of sophistication and in their prices. Some are lightweight, easily mailed and cheap. As mechanical products, they can of course go wrong and so give rise to after-sales problems. Choose a good quality product from the manufacturer who will service and repair faulty equipment.

There are many follow-up possibilities with other safety and security devices, both for the home and the person. The potential market is very large, but the advertiser's problems is to persuade people that they need such products. The problem relates to the typical need/demand distinction (see page 41) that every trader must be clear about. Few people give much thought to their need for security devices until they suffer some misfortune that the device might have prevented. To sell successfully, advertising must bring home to the potential customer the

179

risks he runs, and the relatively small price he need pay to get some measure of protection agains these risks. Well composed display advertising or mailing literature is needed. It is not easy to sell from classified advertising unless you can find a column which specifically appeals to those actively seeking security devices.

Form a clear picture in your mind of your target prospects, and develop a persuasive argument that is relevant to their particular risks and fears. As always, your task is not to describe how wonderful the product is in itself, but to make clear what it can do for the customer. Little old ladies, for example, probably don't want to know that a personal safety device has a 95dB siren; but they may be interested to learn that there's a gadget they can wear unobtrusively on the wrist or round the neck which can enable them to call for help in an emergency.

Food mixers

The mail order attraction of these electric kitchen aids is that your advertising can dwell lovingly on all their detailed functions, whereas the high street shops normally just have the products displayed on the shelves, leaving the customer to guess at precisely what they can do and how they can do it. Shops are also frequently unable to supply the various accessories the manufacturers make – liquidisers, for example, or dough hooks – and the offer of these too can make a mail order package particularly attractive.

Packing and mailing is relatively simple, using manufacturers' cartons with additional packaging if necessary. The main problem is likely to be with after-sales breakdowns or difficulties, and you must be ready to cope with the electrical problems and mechanical failures that will inevitably arise with a percentage of your sales. You will either need your own repair workshop, or should deal with a manufacturer who can speedily service faulty equipment, but even then, you have the work and expense of sending the equipment off for repair and then back to the customer. Your initial selling price must have written into it an adequate sum to cover these contingencies.

Other kitchen aids make suitable follow-ups: electric carving knives, kettles, coffee makers, toasters, and so on, as do other non-electrical kitchen aids.

Furniture

Obviously, the larger and more expensive items of furniture present considerable problems of warehousing and despatch for a mail order operation, but smaller items, particularly those that come in knock-down form, are not especially difficult mail order items. Small tables, bookshelves, firescreens etc are all possibilities.

Because such furniture is readily available in most towns, you will need to give your offer some competitive advantage in the form, for example, of lower prices or unusual design. As always, quality and craftsmanship are difficult to convey in mail order advertising. Perhaps one can only begin to do it by expensive, professionally produced advertising, whose superior quality subliminally suggests the superior quality of the products advertised. It's rather like the thick-pile carpet in the jeweller's shop, which gives the customer a sense of luxury and quality even before he reaches the counter; utility linoleum might cover the floor just as effectively but its message would be quite different. If your advertising budget only runs to the 'cheap lino' kind, stick to low-priced and simple items of furniture.

If you are selling another manufacturer's furniture, he may be able to supply you with advertising literature for you to use unchanged or with only minor modifications.

Follow up with other items of household appeal – ornaments, pictures, rugs, and so on.

Games tables

Full-size conventional tables for snooker or billiards are, of course, very heavy and need substantial warehouse space to store in any quantity, and skilful handling and packing to prepare for despatch. Price/weight ratio, however, is very good. Advertising is probably best done by inviting enquirers to send for your illustrated sales literature. Table tennis tables can be sold in the same way, and are probably a little easier to deal with.

Reduced-size tables are popular for home use, and present fewer problems than full-size models. They may in fact be only table *tops*, designed to sit on a dining table, and these are correspondingly easier to handle.

Related and follow-up sales include all the equipment that players use in these games: cues, balls, marker boards, bats, nets etc. Further possibilities are the main gear and accessories used in other games – tennis, croquet, cricket, golf etc – and books on games of all kinds.

Health foods

There is a large and growing market for so-called health foods of all kinds, and while most towns have a health food shop, or at least a shop that sells such products among others, there is still room for the mail order service to sell to people unable to reach suitable shops and to offer items rarely stocked by the smaller shops.

The price/weight ratio of some staple items is unfortunately not good. The cost of delivering a 1500g pack of wholemeal flour will almost certainly be greater than the price of the flour itself. On the other hand, small packs of herbs and spices have a very good price/weight ratio, and are very easy to handle and mail. Remember also that individually poor price/weight ratio items can often be bulked up to overcome the handicap: a *pack* of something may not be worth considering for mail order, but a *sack* of it may be a different proposition altogether.

The choice of places to advertise is as wide as the market. Magazines devoted to family health, slimmers' magazines and other special interest papers concerned with health or food are obvious places. Most food buyers are women, and so all the women's journals, are possibles, as indeed is the whole of the national press. If you start with an easily described speciality, you could use classified advertising even to sell off the page, eg *PURE BULGARIAN HONEY only £X a 500g jar by post*, or you could invite enquirers to send for your list of specialities – *PURE HONEYS from 40 different countries and 50 different flower species. Send SAE for list.*

Make sure your customers return for further purchases by enclosing order forms and sales literature with all despatched goods. By this means, you can hope to build up a list of regular customers who come back again and again at minimal advertising cost.

Introduction agency

Not the sort of business that can be run on a small scale as you need a sufficiently large number of men and women on your books to justify offering the service in the first place. Your clients must also be geographically close to each other for introductions to be feasible. Such a business as this must leap into existence fully formed. A very large advertising campaign concentrated into a very small period of time and directed at one or more major population centres seems the only way to begin.

Provided you can solve the problem of launching the business and getting enough 'stock on the shelf' virtually instantaneously, such an agency is eminently suited to mail order. Although there clearly has to be a set of principles by which you match one client with another, it comes in the end to a paper-shuffling exercise or its electronic equivalent on a small computer. You need never mail out anything larger than an ordinary letter and your 'stock risk' is nil. The secret is to keep an adequate supply of new clients coming on to the books by continuous large-scale but well directed advertising.

Jewellery

Even cheap jewellery has a very good price/weight ratio for mailing. Many items like rings, earrings, small pendants etc may cost no more to mail than an ordinary letter. For more expensive items, registration may be advisable, but this will still be an acceptably small fraction of total value. Items are easily handled and large stocks may be held in a small space, avoiding the warehousing problems associated with larger and heavier goods. After-sales problems should be minimal, and the follow-up possibilities of selling further items of jewellery to satisfied customers are good.

The real problem is how to advertise. Well illustrated display advertising is essential for off-the-page selling, and well produced sales literature is needed to send to enquirers. Only the very simplest items can be offered in classified advertising with any hope of success, eg plain 9ct gold wedding rings.

If you are a jewellery manufacturer of cheap items, you could offer jewellery in bulk lots by mail to market traders, party planners and others. Advertise in the market trade papers. Or if your work is of a higher quality and in more expensive materials, you could offer it to established retail jewellers by direct mailing them, but again you will need high quality advertising literature.

Retailing other manufacturers' jewellery is difficult because of the large number of shops in every town which sell jewellery, most of them with extensive window displays. That's where your competition lies, and you will need to make your mail order offer particularly attractive if you are to sell profitably direct to the public.

Keep-fit equipment
Rowing machines, exercise bicycles, dumb-bells, sunbeds, sunlamps – there are large numbers of gadgets and pieces of equipment which appeal to the keep-fit enthusiast. For some, the mail order appeal of such items is their local unavailability; for others, it is the anonymity of the transaction – buying by post is less embarrassing than buying in person.

The price range of different sorts of keep-fit equipment is very wide, so you should be able to choose items appropriate to the sort of advertising you want to undertake. Naturally, the cheaper or more basic items can more easily be sold off-the-page than the more expensive or more complicated ones, which need good display advertising and mailing literature. After-sales problems depend very much on the equipment concerned; there is not much that can go wrong with a set of weights, for example, but other items with moving or electrical components can give rise to problems.

Kitchen utensils
The attraction of kitchen utensils for the mail order dealer is that every household is a potential target. Saucepans, frying pans etc sold as

matching sets can be promoted either as useful gifts or for the purchaser's own use.

Detail the qualities for cooking purposes of the particular materials the pans are made of, stressing how easy it is to use and to clean them and how they enhance the excellence of whatever is being cooked – or whatever their virtues really are. High street shops tend to display their kitchenware in a rather unhelpful manner, leaving potential buyers with little upon which to base their buying decisions beyond appearance and price. Mail order can score by talking informatively to the intelligent cook.

Price/weight ratio is good for sets of items, and sometimes acceptable even for single items. After-sales problems should be few.

A well produced catalogue of items can be advertised in the classified columns. Particular items or sets can be sold off the page by well designed display advertising.

Follow-up possibilities include the complete range of kitchenware in particular and of household items in general.

Knock-down industrial-type furniture

Almost all businesses and many homes are targets for offers of heavy-duty shelving and storage systems that bolt solid steel units together. Obviously these are very heavy items, and so delivery has to be by a carrier other than the Post Office.

After-sales problems are almost nil as, provided you have delivered the right units with the right number of nuts and bolts and instructions for assembly, there is virtually nothing to go wrong.

The mail order appeal, particularly for the domestic customer wanting shelving for a garage or workshop, is that such items are not readily available in high street shops, and the manufacturers who supply direct to industry are not usually interested in small orders for individual items from members of the public.

There are no obvious follow-ups for the domestic buyer, though business buyers, of course, will need more storage equipment as their businesses grow. It could be worth re-mailing customers annually.

Display advertising, particularly for shelving with special features, is probably better than classified advertising inviting enquiries.

The product being very heavy and bulky, this is no business for the weak or infirm or for traders without adequate warehouse space.

Made-to-measure clothes

This is a service business which at first sight seems an impossible one to run by mail. Yet there are mail order businesses which have been offering such a service for years, advertising for clients by the simplest of classified ads in the national press.

You need to define the service you offer very clearly. Men's clothing is preferable to ladies' clothing because it is less subject to the vagaries of fashion. There are two ways of offering the service, and both may be used at the same time. Offer to make up shirts, for example, or trousers or suits either by inviting clients to send you an old garment which you undertake to copy in a material of their choice, or by asking the client to supply you with detailed measurements from which you make a finished garment to the client's chosen pattern and in his chosen material.

The more you can standardise the service, the easier it will be for you. You need to stock some materials and must be able to supply returnable sets of specimen materials from which your customers can choose. The narrower the choice, the easier your stock and supply problem, but the less attractive your service to clients; striking the right balance is one of the required skills.

Goods are easily packed and mailed with a good price/weight ratio. Provided you are a competent tailor, after-sales problems should be few, and such as there are should be easy for you to deal with.

Follow-ups include the sale of other clothes – possibly including ready-made clothes – and a repair and alterations service for clients' existing clothes.

Mini washing machines
The mini-washing machine doesn't normally spring to mind when one is considering what to sell by mail, but it is typical of a whole range of products eminently suited to mail order selling. It is genuinely useful, and its small size makes it both unusual, giving it a slightly gadgety appeal, and far easier to handle and despatch than a full-size machine.

You need suitable warehouse space and the means to deal with after-sales problems, which are inevitable in a product called upon to produce and withstand energetic mechanical action.

Although the obvious consumable for washing machines is washing powder, that is a product whose price/weight ratio rules it out as a mail order possibility. The follow-ups to consider are other small-scale household items: small vacuum cleaners, carpet sweepers, rugs, electric kettles, and so on.

Office stationery
Envelopes, computer stationery, carbon paper, typing and printer ribbons, pens, pencils, adhesive tape, staples, duplicating and photo-copying supplies, record cards etc – there is not a business in the land which does not need a regular supply of at least some of these items and

others like them. Note that these are all unprinted items, entirely standard, and can be shipped without individual processing between your receipt of supplies from manufacturer or wholesaler and your despatch of them to retail customers. Bulked-up supplies – which is what you will be dealing in – can make quite large and heavy cartons, and you may have to use non-Post Office delivery services for many of your sales.

Being consumables, office stationery items have the attraction to the mail trader of building up a business which, if successful, quickly acquires a certain momentum: satisfied customers keep coming back for more. And as these supplies are the necessities of life for a business, not optional extras like most consumer products sold by mail, you've a higher than usual chance of getting a customer for life.

Advertising need not be elaborate or expensive. A small classified ad in the right place, eg appropriate trade and professional journals, inviting enquiries for your office stationery price-list may be all that you need. Bear in mind also that as you are seeking long-term continuing customers, you can afford to take a short-term loss on your initial advertising and sales if this seems a good way of pulling in a reasonable number of customers to get the business going. This is not to say that you should go for a short-term loss as a matter of policy, but you certainly have it as an option if it seems appropriate.

Outdoor wear

Motorcycle jackets, flying jackets, raincoats etc are always popular mail order lines. Though often bulky, their price/weight ratio is generally good, and they should not cause any problems in mailing. Government surplus gear can often be offered at keen prices which undercut similar garments selling in high street shops. Of course, to acquire the government surplus or similar stock you need to buy in quantity at auctions and you therefore need adequate warehousing to store your goods. Alternatively, if you buy stock through a local wholesaler you can work with a smaller stock but almost certainly at less advantageous prices.

Items like these can be sold off the page by display advertising or via classified ads if you invite enquirers to send for your catalogue.

After-sales problems should be minimal. Follow-ups of other items of clothing and footwear should appeal to satisfied customers. Go for the camping/walking/climbing market, and possibly include non-clothing items of related interest in your catalogue – tents, backpacks, outdoor stoves, and so on.

Party novelties

Fancy hats, balloons, streamers, crackers, decorations etc are all basically cheap items bought infrequently and in quantities that are too small to support a mail order business – if, that is, you try to sell exclusively to the general public. A venture with more profit potential is to wholesale such items to market traders, shops and major users such as hotels and restaurants at Christmas/New Year and other special occasions.

Party novelties are easy to pack and mail, and after-sales problems should be nil. If you do indeed supply to the trade, repeat orders are likely from satisfied customers.

Once you have established outlets with market traders, follow-up possibilities are limitless: anything that market traders sell would make a reasonable addition to your range of products – cheap reproduction pictures, toys, games, ornaments, gadgets of all kinds and so on.

If you also plan to sell direct to the public, this side of the business should concentrate on those items that are more expensive in small quantities – fancy dress costumes, for example, conjuring tricks, sets of toys, games and so on. By all means try to sell the cheaper items to the public too, but only as additions to the more costly sales.

Photograph display products

Frames, large and small, cheap and expensive, albums, pocket wallets etc are all easy to handle and mail, though advertising needs to be illustrated if the customer is to be tempted to buy. As always with fairly commonplace, widely available products, the mail trader must offer something out of the ordinary either by way of price or specification. For example, frames can be offered monogrammed with the buyer's initials, or albums can be personalised with titles in gold letters like *My Holiday in Venice* or *The Smith Family Over the Years* or whatever else the customer specifies.

Follow-up possibilities include everything related to the taking, processing and display of photographs: a developing and printing service, special enlargements (poster-size prints of customers' favourite photographs?), cameras and other photographic equipment etc.

An alternative way forward is to specialise in frames and framing, and to move on from the cheaper small display items to larger and more elaborate frames suitable for paintings or reproductions of paintings. This could be a made-to-measure service; or you could supply easily assembled frames in knock-down form, the latter being cheaper and easier to mail and handle.

None of these items should cause any after-sales problems in the ordinary way.

Printing

A printing service can very effectively be offered by mail. Small items like business cards, self-adhesive labels, compliment slips etc make convenient mail order items with a good price/weight ratio. Businesses need regular supplies of printed stationery of all kinds so an established printing business with an adequate supply of satisfied customers can be a worthwhile venture, less dependent on continuous advertising than businesses without this built-in likelihood of repeat orders.

To get repeat orders, of course, you not only need satisfied customers, you also need your customers to have successful businesses which steadily use up their stationery and so need to come back to you for replenishment. Bearing this in mind, pitch your advertising at established businesses rather than at business beginners. Although there are a good number of the latter in the market, many of them will fail to re-order simply because their own businesses have not survived. If your business is aimed solely at business newcomers, you will be continuously trawling for new customers and getting very little repeat business.

Follow-up possibilities are many: duplicate books, letterheads, advertising calendars, advertising diaries etc. There are also the related fields of rubber stamps and printed advertising promotions like ball pens, key fobs, bookmarks etc. And if you wished, you could follow up with unprinted stationery - envelopes, packing materials, account books - and other business requisites.

Refuse sacks and polythene sheeting

In your search for products to sell by mail, do remember - as the above paragraphs illustrated - that mail order may be used just as effectively selling to business and industry as to the general public. While it would be impossible to run a viable mail order business selling refuse sacks and polythene sheeting in small quantities to householders, it is certainly possible to build a successful business supplying such items in lots of a thousand or more to business and industry. Advertise in appropriate trade journals or direct mail your offer to suitable firms.

For large quantities, the price/weight ratio is favourable, and packaging and despatch present no problems, though you will probably have to use carriers other than the Post Office. After-sales problems should be minimal, and the follow-up possibilities just more of the same. If you wish to develop your product range, you could move into packaging - both in plastics and other materials - and packing machinery.

Rugs

In terms of handling, mailing and after-sales problems, rugs make convenient products to sell by mail. The difficulty lies in advertising a low-cost product which needs to be well-illustrated to attract sales. If the rugs you sell have some special characteristic, this may be highlighted in your advertising, and so make your problem simpler. For example, your rugs may be specially fire-resistant or stain-resistant or easily washable. But even with such characteristics, you still need to illustrate the product, choosing between off-the-page selling through display advertising, and sending iillustrated sales literature to enquirers responding to your classified advertising.

Follow-up possibilities include the full range of household products.

Scientific equipment and materials

The basic equipment of laboratory research is available over the counter from only the most specialist suppliers, very thinly spread over the country. Test tubes, beakers, flasks, pipettes, thermometers, and so on, are as vital to the small or home-based amateur laboratory as to the largest industrial laboratories. The latter have no difficulty in getting supplies, but the former often do, and for them a mail order service is a boon.

Much of the paraphernalia of the laboratory is either breakable, consumable or has a very short life, and your satisfied customers will need to come back to you repeatedly. Follow-ups also include the more permanent and expensive pieces of equipment – microscopes, lasers, spectroscopes etc.

Advertise in the relevant special interest journals, inviting enquirers to send for your list of supplies. If at first you restrict yourself to the simpler things like test tubes, indicator paper, wash bottles and so on, an elaborate catalogue is not vital as these things need only be named – sometimes with measurements – to be understood.

The more fragile items require careful packaging, and some breakages in transit must be expected, but once in the hands of your customers, none of the basic laboratory equipment and materials should cause any after-sales problems.

Screws, nuts, bolts, nails etc

DIY enthusiasts and various tradespeople use vast quantities of fixings and fastenings so that although the unit cost of each item is tiny, mail order sales of large packs can make a worthwhile business.

Advertising is straightforward. The customer knows what he wants, and all you need to do is list the nature and sizes of the items you supply together with their quantity prices. Mailing is easy, after-sales problems should be nil, and follow-up orders should keep coming from old customers, provided you maintain a speedy service at a fair price.

Once you have built a good customer list and have a firm basis for a continuing business, you can think of promoting other items of DIY and practical interest to your customers – screwdrivers, drills and other tools, for example. Enclose advertising literature on these other items when fulfilling orders.

Seeds

Most packets of seeds, whether of flower or vegetables, weigh very little indeed and their price/weight ratio is excellent. Packing and mailing could hardly be easier, and the risk of damage in transit is negligible. From the customer's point of view, the mail order appeal must lie in something out of the ordinary in your offer, as packets of seeds are widely available, and keen gardeners swap seeds and cuttings among themselves without resort to the commercial seedsman.

There are various ways in which you could make your offer a special one. You could, for example, draw up plans for garden plots of different sizes, and suggest precisely how a variety of different seeds should be sown in order to obtain certain effects; in such a case, your offer would consist of the plan, full instructions, and all the packets of seeds required. Or you could simply make up bumper packs of packets of different varieties of seeds, carefully chosen for their attractiveness when grown together, and offer these at an all-in price. Or you could specialise in unusual seeds or ones that are not easy to find in local garden centres.

A well produced full-colour catalogue would be helpful, but there is no reason why you should not be able to sell direct from classified advertising, or from lists of seeds sent to enquirers.

The follow-up possibilities are not difficult to work out: satisfied customers will come back year after year for their annuals, and you could move on from packets of seeds to bushes and trees, although these are naturally much more difficult to handle. Other items of interest for gardeners, from lawnmowers to fencing, from soil-testing sets to secateurs, could also be offered. Direct mail your customer list every year in good time for the spring sowing.

Sportswear

Track suits, running shoes, football boots, cricket gear, boxing shorts etc are among the large range of sportswear goods that may be offered by mail. The market is a large one, and the more all-purpose items like track suits can be successfully advertised in the national press, while the more specialist items, eg judo gear, mountaineering clothing, are best advertised in the specialist journals for enthusiasts.

Sportswear gives little handling or mailing difficulty to the dealer. The price/weight ratio is good.

Follow up with other items of sporting interest – sports equipment, books on sport, camping equipment etc.

As with many of the more popular areas of mail trading, if you can find a product with slightly unusual characteristics which can be written up and illustrated in order to bring out the product's uniqueness and usefulness, you have a very good starting point for a mail order business.

Stamps

The 'approval' method of selling stamps by post is very well established. Probably the best and cheapest way of acquiring stock for resale is to buy private collections, either direct from the public or at auction, though it is possible to buy stamps in presentation packs from certain suppliers and, of course, if you are interested in dealing in current UK stamps and the many commemoratives issued, you can buy them across the counter at face value at any post office at the time of issue. The Post Office also provides facilities for acquiring cleanly postmarked first day covers.

Of all items sold by mail, there is probably nothing lighter, simpler to pack, or cheaper to mail than postage stamps. All serious collectors are familiar with the main catalogues which list virtually every stamp and variant form of every stamp that has ever existed, so the small dealer need not print expensive catalogues himself. He need merely give the details of a stamp, and collectors will be able to identify it and know what it looks like.

At the junk end of the market – by no means to be despised by the dealer – are the large packs of various stamps which appeal to the new young collector. At the top end of the market, there are individual stamps changing hands – which probably means moving from one owner's bank vault to another owner's bank vault – at thousands of pounds a time. The new mail order dealer will probably find it best to start his venture at the lower end of the market.

Follow-up possibilities are, of course, stamps and more stamps. If you sell by the approval method, your aim is to get regular customers who buy from you over and over again. Other follow-ups include stamp albums, catalogues, magnifying glasses and all the other aids the collector uses.

Tableware sets

Everyone needs cups, saucers, plates, knives, forks etc, and all these things are readily available in high street shops. The mail order dealer must have something unique to offer customers – an unusual design, a free gift, a low price etc.

China and glass are, of course, easily broken, so packaging must be done carefully. Some sets of tableware come prepacked in manufacturers' presentation cases, and though these may themselves need to be packed securely in outer boxes, they can simplify your handling problems. As always, the higher the quality of your product, the greater the problem of advertising but the fewer your other problems. A cheaply printed design that starts to fade in the first wash may, because of complaints and returned goods, give rise to greater costs than you would have had if you had purchased a more expensive but better product in the first place, even if you went on to sell it at the same price as the inferior product. Given a product of adequate quality, there should be few after-sales problems beyond the inevitable breakages in transit, and these, of course, must be allowed for in your pricing.

Follow-up possibilities include tablecloths/napkins, kitchen utensils and household goods in general.

Telephone equipment

Advances in technology and the relaxation of British Telecom's tight control over apparatus that may be plugged into the telephone system has opened up a large market in telephone-linked devices. Answering machines, call recorders, cordless phones, call diverters, memory phones, phone amplifiers – devices like these, together with a much wider variety of telephone shapes and sizes, are now available and the demand for them is still growing.

All these devices make good items for mail order. Although problems of reliability and after-sales difficulties must be expected, the products have a lot in their favour for mail order selling. Product prices are high enough to justify the cost of well produced advertising. Most products can be excitingly written up at length, detailing the various features they offer. There has always been a 'useless gadgets' section of the mail order market, appealing to those whose sense of wonder at what things can do is stronger than their judgement as to the necessity of doing them. Telephone devices appeal directly to this market. But they appeal also to the coolheaded, calculating business person who can see worthwhile applications for such things. So there are two different markets to go for, and the follow-up possibilities will be different in the two markets. The buyers of gadgets will be interested in more gadgets, electronic or otherwise; the business market will be interested in other business equipment and business services that are demonstrably cost-effective.

Before purchasing equipment for resale, satisfy yourself as to its acceptability to British Telecom, its reliability, and the manufacturer's back-up service.

Towels

Towels have many desirable features from the mail trader's point of view. They are easy to pack, no problem to handle, and most unlikely to be damaged in transit. Unless they are defective in manufacture, which they should not be if you have chosen them carefully, there is virtually nothing to go wrong with them after sale. Satisfied customers can be tempted with further household textiles – curtains, bedding, rugs are obvious examples – or more specifically with other towelling items: bath robes, beach robes, nappies, face flannels, tea towels, and so on. Even the smallest household needs several towels of different sizes and shapes, so the market is a very large one.

But, of course, like all large markets, it is already well supplied. The question to which you must find a convincing answer is why anyone should buy towels by mail when the nearest high street may have dozens of shops which stock them.

For single items, at least, you will almost certainly not be able to compete on price because even lower-quality towels are reasonably heavy and the price/weight ratio of a cheap towel leads to an unfavourably high postal cost. But what about *sets* of towels? Half a dozen hand towels, for example, or a family set of hand towels and bath towels. The price/weight ratio improves as the order becomes larger. Or you might consider personalised towels, monogrammed with the customer's initials; or gift packs, perhaps with bubble bath sachets or scented soap included – just the thing for Christmas, or Mother's Day, or birthdays.

Advertising really needs to illustrate the product, preferably in good quality colour to suggest the quality of the towels. Trying to sell off the page from classified ads is unlikely to succeed.

Typing

The typing of students' theses, authors' manuscripts and other lengthy documents can form the basis of a viable mail order business, particularly if you can offer it in association with some other skill, such as fluency in the less common foreign languages, or the ability to cope with mathematical and scientific data, or a familiarity with medical or legal phraseology. Like most services, the typing service causes few problems in mailing because it is the expertise that is being sold rather than the related physical material. Even extensive and bulky typescripts make up into small parcels and are very easy to pack and mail.

To offer the service, you need to be a skilled typist with a good quality typewriter, certainly with a carbon ribbon and preferably with interchangeable typeheads so that different styles can be offered. A microcomputer with a word processing program and a high quality printer would be eminently suitable, permitting even a less-than-perfect typist to produce perfect copy if prepared to take the trouble to check and correct as necessary.

Advertise in student papers, the more intellectual journals, and papers read by actual or would-be writers.

Follow-up possibilities include anything that may be typed – letters, curricula vitae, master copies of newsletters and so on. And the business could branch out into the related fields of duplicating and photocopying.

Start-up costs for this, as for most mail order service businesses, are low, provided you already have the equipment. What you mainly need is expertise of a moderately high order if you are seriously to consider this type of business. Little is needed in the way of stock beyond a supply of paper and typing ribbons.

A word of caution: typing is a widely held skill and there are a large number of practitioners competing in the market.

Unusual and expensive foods

Although there is a seasonal spurt in the market for unusual and expensive foods as Christmas approaches, it is possible to establish a business with a sufficiently regular clientele to keep it going throughout the year. The requirement is that your product should appeal to the self-indulgent, and not merely to those who wish to indulge their relatives and friends. Special chocolates, sweets, cheeses, biscuits etc can appeal to the buyer for his own consumption, while mixed packs of foods in presentation but re-usable hampers can be offered to the gift market.

Nothing is as consumable as food, and with an adequate supply of satisfied and regular clients you should be able to run a successful business. Advertise in the up-market papers and magazines.

Price/weight ratio is good, and mailing should not be a problem once you have worked out a suitable packaging for your product. Some items may be subject to damage in transit, and with perishable items there is always the risk of decay. But these occupational hazards can be allowed for in your pricing, and need not deter you if you think you have a product or products sufficiently expensive and of wide enough appeal.

As with all consumables, the follow-up is more of the same.

Video hire

The mailability of cassettes was mentioned earlier, and naturally the same considerations apply here. A video club, hiring out pre-recorded tapes for a fixed period, is a natural 'repeat' business, the customers coming again and again as part of the basic business deal.

You might charge an annual subscription plus so much a loan, and it would also be prudent to require a deposit against the non-return or damage of goods.

Your major cost is in the setting up and maintenance of a good library of tapes, but if you do your costing properly, this could turn into a profitable venture once you have sold a reasonable number of subscriptions, at least until the public libraries move into the business.

Watches

Quartz watches are very reliable, keep excellent time, and are very convenient for mail order selling. The price/weight ratio is very good and mailing in padded envelopes is safe and reliable. The mail trader's difficulty is that watches are very widely sold and you must have a very special inducement to persuade people to buy by mail. A well produced and illustrated catalogue of a large number of watches from the very cheap to the ridiculously expensive could be just such an inducement if offered free to enquirers, though this would, of course, necessitate your having to hold an extensive and costly stock.

Since a very high standard of timekeeping is now available in the cheapest watches, people only buy more expensive ones if they offer a range of other functions beyond simply telling the time, or if they are of superior design – and this is where your illustrated catalogue may prove a winner. Let the illustrations show the various watch faces, straps and bracelets clearly. For the multi-function watches, detail in full all the things the watch does and give examples of the circumstances in which such functions may be used.

Wines

The wine market has grown enormously in recent years, and despite all the high street off-licences, a large amount of business is now done by mail order. To succeed, you must be able to find good value-for-money wines in this country, or, preferably, to import them yourself. Either of these ways of acquiring stock implies the need for genuine knowledge of wines and the wine market.

Your customers will buy from you if they find your choices are to their taste and suit their pocket, so you must be able to satisfy them on a continuing basis. You may succeed in selling the odd case of poor quality wine, but your customers will never re-order – and that, as with all consumables, is what you're really aiming at.

You will need a certain amount of cellar space, and the handling of cases of wine is not of course an occupation for the frail or infirm. But cartons are regularly shaped, though heavy, and are not difficult to handle. You will have to use carriers other than the Post Office as cases of wine are not suitable for the mail.

The market is a large and a growing one, but it is also increasingly competitive. It is not a business for the well meaning amateur, but the

195

real wine buff with the ability to identify good wines and purchase them shrewdly could do well.

Women's ready-to-wear clothes
Women's wear is the single largest product area in contemporary mail order. The range is enormous, from sensible shoes to outrageous underwear, with dresses, skirts, blouses, coats etc in between. Almost all are lightweight and easy to mail, with virtually nothing to get damaged in transit and little to give rise to after-sales problems, provided the products are well made.

Advertising usually needs to include good illustrations, so selling off the page can be expensive. Instead, you could produce good quality sales literature to send to enquirers prompted by lower cost advertising.

The market is, of course, both large and already well served, so you need to find a competitive edge. The particular mail order appeal may lie in low prices, unusual design, unusual sizes – very large, very small – and the chance to try things on at home and be able to return unsuitable items without fuss or difficulty.

Not least, there is the element of sheer *fun* – looking forward to the parcel of goodies and watching out for the postman until they come. Is this perhaps the greatest mail order appeal of all – that it makes us briefly like small children again, experiencing once more something of the excited anticipation of Christmas Eves of long ago?

Appendix 2

Addresses

Advertising Association
Abford House, 15 Wilton Road, London SW1V 1NJ; 071-828 2771
Advertising Standards Authority
Brook House, 2–16 Torrington Place, London WC1E 7HN; 071-580 5555
Audit Bureau of Circulations
Black Prince Yard, 207 High Street, Berkhamsted, Herts HP4 1AD; 0442 870800
British Market Research Bureau
53 The Mall, London W5 3TE; 081-567 3060
British Rate and Data
Maclean Hunter Ltd, Maclean House, Chalk Lane, Cockfosters Road, Barnet, Herts EN4 0BU; 081-975 9759
CACI Ltd
CACI House, Kensington Village, Avonmore Road, London W14 8TS; 071-602 6000
Code of Advertising Practice Committee
Brook House, 2–16 Torrington Place, London WC1E 7HN; 071-580 5555
Data Protection Registrar
Springfield House, Water Lane, Wilmslow, Cheshire SK9 5AX; 0625 535777
Direct Mail Information Service
5 Carlisle Street, London W1V 5RG; 071-494 0483
Direct Mail Services Standards Board
26 Eccleston Street, London SW1W 9PY; 071-824 8651
Direct Marketing Association
1st Floor, 199 Knightsbridge, London SW7 1RP; 071-233 9168
Her Majesty's Stationery Office
PO Box 276, London SW8 5DT; 071-873 9090
Incorporated Society of British Advertisers
44 Hertford Street, London W1Y 8AE; 071-499 7502
Institute of Practitioners in Advertising
44 Belgrave Square, London SW1X 8QS; 071-235 7020

Joint Industry Committee for National Readership Surveys
44 Belgrave Square, London SW1X 8QS; 071-235 7020

Mail Order Traders' Association
100 Old Hall Street, Liverpool L3 9TD; 051-227 4181

Mail Users' Association
3 Pavement House, The Pavement, Hay-on-Wye, Hereford HR3 5BU; 0497 821357

Mailing Preference Service
1 Leeward House, Plantation Wharf, London SW11 3TY; 071-738 1625

National Newspapers' Mail Order Protection Scheme
16 Tooks Court, London EC4A 1LB; 071-405 6806

Newspaper Society
Bloomsbury House, 74–77 Great Russell Street, London WC1B 3DA; 071-636 7014

Office of Fair Trading
Field House, 15–25 Bream's Buildings, London EC4A 1PR; 071-242 2858

Periodical Publishers Association
Imperial House, 15–19 Kingsway, London WC2B 6UN; 071-379 6268

Post Office Headquarters
30 St James's Square, London SW1Y 4PY; 071-490 2888

Post Office Users' National Council
Waterloo Bridge House, Waterloo Road, London SE1 8UA; 071-928 9458

Royal Mail
Direct Marketing Dept, Room 221, Royal Mail House, 148–166 Old Street, London EC1V 9HQ; 071-250 2351

Scottish Daily Newspaper Society
30 Georges Square, Glasgow G2 1EG; 041-248 2375

Scottish Newspaper Publishers Association
48 Palmerston Place, Edinburgh EH12 5DE; 031-220 4353

Appendix 3

Bibliography

The titles marked * below are referred to in the main text of the book – check titles in the Index for page references. Some of these titles are out of print but should still be available from your local library.

Reading

Andrews, Les *The Guide to Effective Direct Mail* (Post Office) 1985
Andrews, Les (ed) *The Post Office Direct Mail Handbook* (Exley) 1984
*Bird, Drayton *Commonsense Direct Marketing* 2nd edition (Kogan Page) 1989
*Brann, Christian *Direct Mail & Direct Response Promotion* (Kogan Page) 1971.
Corby, M & Fairlie R *The Mail Users' Handbook* (Fairlie & Corby) 1984
Fairlie, Robin *Direct Mail Principles and Practice* (Kogan Page) 1979
Hughes, John *The Mail Marketing File* (Mail Marketing (Bristol) Ltd) 1983
Jefkins, Frank *Advertisement Writing* (Macdonald & Evans) 1976
Jefkins, Frank *Advertising* (Macdonald & Evans) 1985
Nicholl, D S *Advertising: Its Purpose, Principles and Practice* (Macdonald & Evans) 1978
*Patten, Dave *Successful Marketing for the Small Business: the Daily Telegraph Guide* 2nd edition (Kogan Page) 1988

Reference

The following titles are usually published annually unless otherwise indicated:

Advertisers Annual (Reed Information Services Ltd)
BRAD Direct Marketing (Maclean Hunter) twice yearly
British Code of Advertising Practice (CAP) 1988
British Code of Sales Promotion Practice (CAP) 1984
British Rate and Data (Maclean Hunter) monthly
Direct Marketing Services (Benn)
Handbook of Recognised Agencies (DMSSB)

*Kelly's Manufacturers and Merchants Directory (Kelly's)
*Letraset catalogue (Esselte Letraset)
Rules for Direct Marketing Including List & Database Management (CAP)
 1991
*Whitaker's Almanack (Whitaker)
*Willing's Press Guide (Reed Information Services Ltd)

Further Reading from Kogan Page

Do It Yourself Advertising, Roy Brewer, 1991
A Handbook of Advertising Techniques, Tony Harrison, 2nd edn, 1989
How to Increase Sales Without Leaving Your Desk, Edmund Tirbutt, 1991
How to Make Exhibitions Work for Your Business, John Talbot, 1989
How to Market Books, Alison Baverstock, 1990
Law for the Small Business, Patricia Clayton, 7th edn, 1991
Readymade Business Letters, Jim Dening, 1988
Readymade Job Advertisements, Neil Wenborn, 1991
The Small Business Action Kit, John Rosthorn *et al*, 3rd edn, 1991

Index

uniqueness 40
upper case 123

Value Added Tax 63, 67
VAT *see* Value Added Tax
visualiser 125
visuals 97

Whitaker's Almanack 95, 200

Willing's Press Guide 135, 200
working from home 13, 70
write-ups 110

Yellow Pages 69, 96

zero-rated supplies 64

* Eventions
001 - 404 521 1846

Tonya